Unfinished Business

David Love was born in 1933, gained a degree in economics from the Australian National University, and went on to head the *Australian Financial Review*'s Canberra office in the early 1960s. After working for the World Bank in Washington, and taking on the simultaneous jobs of economics editor with the AFR and economics leader writer with the *Sydney Morning Herald*, he established Syntec, a highly regarded, privately circulated monthly newsletter that analysed business and financial developments for its high-level subscribers. John Fairfax & Sons took a half-share in the business in the mid-1980s, but Love eventually bought out their share, finally selling the business to Access Economics in 1998. Love is also the author of *Straw Polls, Paper Money* (2001).

For Pamela, my wife of 50 years

Unfinished Business

Paul Keating's interrupted revolution

David Love

Scribe Publications
18–20 Edward St, Brunswick, Victoria 3056, Australia

First published by Scribe 2008
Reprinted 2008
This edition published 2009
Reprinted 2019, 2020, 2021, 2022

Typeset in Granjon by the publishers

Printed and bound in Australia by Griffin Press

Scribe is committed to the sustainable use of natural resources and the use of paper products made responsibly from those resources.

Scribe acknowledges Australia's First Nations peoples as the traditional owners and custodians of this country, and we pay our respects to their elders, past and present.

978 1 921640 14 8 (Australian edition)

A catalogue record for this book is available from the National Library of Australia.

scribepublications.com.au

Contents

‘Solanio: Now, what news on the Rialto?’
–*The Merchant of Venice*, William Shakespeare

The city of Venice was a wonder of late medieval and renaissance Europe, and at its heart was the Rialto district, site of a remarkable international money-market embodying institutional banking, commercial-bills trading, bond trading, and foreign-exchange dealing.

Introduction

SINCE RELINQUISHING THE OFFICE OF PRIME MINISTER OF Australia, Paul Keating has chosen to operate as an acidic commentator on people and politics. It is a stance that has allowed both the Liberal–National Party coalition and the Australian Labor Party to dismiss him as an eccentric. Worse, for most of its recent period in government, the coalition was left free to peddle the myth that his prime ministership had bequeathed them an economy and a set of policies badly in need of repair, while the left wing of the Labor Party moaned that he had left them nothing of value.

This situation is astonishing because, at the point that Australians voted his government out of office in 1996, Keating was more than halfway towards completing the most sweeping and beneficial set of changes in financial policy, financial engineering, and social policy attempted in any democracy during the 20th century. Thanks to his achievements, Australia was transformed from an imminent candidate for the title of 'the white trash of Asia' to a nation whose economy and financial services industry were the envy of the region.

Yet, because his achievements were largely in the financial area, there has been a tendency to regard Keating's reforms as off the radar of ordinary folk. And it has suited most of those who are aware of his ambitions and achievements to keep it that way. When I spoke to David Clarke, founder of Macquarie Bank, before the 2007 election, he was careful—like other financial leaders—not to say anything that would favour Paul Keating over John Howard. Clarke was one of Howard's Sydney coterie. But without Keating's reforms during the middle to late 1980s, Macquarie Bank would not have enjoyed the climate and framework of policies and markets that allowed the bank to become the spectacular success it has. Indeed, there might not have been a Macquarie Bank (whose name has since changed to Macquarie Group).

I was drawn to write this book because of my interest in the parallel evolution of Paul Keating under the tutelage of people like Ted Evans—now chairman of Westpac Bank, but once head of the Treasury—and of a smart operation called Hill Samuel Australia, which became the much more stupendous Macquarie Group. One of the fascinations of the topic is the political environment in which the developments described here took place: a left-wing government was spearheading a dramatic right-wing change in policies sufficiently radical to allow the emergence of new capitalist institutions.

At first, I thought I would be content to draw a couple of newspaper articles out of this material, but I discovered the story was much bigger. As I researched further, I became increasingly aware of what you might call an ancillary force that soon became the over-riding principal impetus for change. I am referring here to the industrial pensions movement, which Keating and Bill Kelty, secretary of the Australian Council of Trade Unions from

1983 to 1999, brought from conception into infancy and primed for growth. In the gestation of this superannuation, Keating was perhaps no more important than others. But from his privileged vantage point in the national leadership, he threw the patronage of government policy over the industrial superannuation funds and established them as the keys to Australia's future economic performance.

Keating's genius was to perceive a complex mix of politics, economics, market initiatives, and social policy as an interactive combination that formed an organic whole. The former Labor prime minister to me evokes an ancient shade: a trader calling from the Rialto. A combination of positive domestic and international market forces similar to those that created renaissance Venice emerged with remarkable effect in Australia in the 1980s and 1990s. The Venetian strain is still running, but it ran best in the 1990s as it carried the country to economic safety through a period when predators smashed currencies, markets, and economies to our immediate north. The hedge funds that did this thought they would do the same in Australia, but instead went away with bloodied noses.

The first part of this book is the story of 30 years of extraordinary activity that went largely unnoticed by the public; of entrepreneurial ability that unfolded in both the public and private spheres against a broader context of cosy, complacent financial institutions and a parliamentary culture that was conservative and backward-looking. It leads us through the defeat of the international hedge funds in the 1990s and the contemporary sub-prime mortgages crisis. The second part of this book concerns how a superb politician of a kind seen only once in a lifetime came to be cast off as a whimsical lightweight, how his economic policy legacy to the nation was almost squandered; and how it may yet be saved.

Part I
Out to the Rialto

Chapter 1

The Ancient Regime

IT SEEMS ONLY YESTERDAY, WHEN WE WERE HICKS: IT WAS 1986. I had bumped into an acquaintance from school days on the street in Sydney. We were not close friends, but we had played rugby together and had shared sufficiently fond memories to go off for a drink. I told him I had become a specialist in financial economics. After a career as a senior journalist on various Australian newspapers, I had been awarded a State Department scholarship to the United States. A period working for the World Bank in Washington DC had followed, and now I was back in Australia working as a consultant.

For his part, he had stayed at home at his parents' rural property in northern New South Wales and now ran the place.

He proceeded to tell me the tale of a young dairy farmer from his district. A chance had come up for this man to buy a neighbouring property. But he would have to borrow, and bank interest rates were then well into double digits.

The young farmer had heard somewhere that Swiss currency loans were to be had for maybe 4 per cent interest. His local bank manager had agreed to look into this for him. The bank manager came back to say that, yes, he'd had his people check it out; a Swiss franc borrowing, not as low as 4 per cent, but certainly much lower than Australian rates, could be had. With the farm as collateral, it would be fine. It was a marvellous opportunity.

Things went well until the bank manager suddenly appeared at the young farmer's home to say that there had been a major revaluation of the Swiss franc relative to the Australian dollar and the farmer's repayment was now more than his farm was worth.

'The thing became notorious in the district,' my friend said. 'The farmer went bankrupt. And the respected bank manager became reviled. He had betrayed an aspiring young man. Can you tell me how this could have happened?'

'Well, I don't know the incident, but you say the borrowing was uncovered,' I said. 'Do you know what that means?'

'Well, er, vaguely …'

'It means that, at the time of the foreign-exchange borrowing, the borrower and his bank had not set up a protection to allow the young farmer to pay back the Swiss francs on exactly the terms he had bought them for. And, you know, the cost of covering would have brought the interest rate on the Swiss loan up to the interest-rate cost of a borrowing in domestic Australian terms.'

'Shouldn't the bank manager have known this?'

'He should have, but apparently he didn't. Let me give you a short lecture. Do you mind?'

'No. I'd very much value it.'

'Well, accept first that everything has a yield. Your property has a yield arrived at by taking the income you get from it as a percentage of your property's market value. My home has a yield set by taking the rent I could get for it as a percentage of its market value. If the market value goes up the yield drops, because it is now a lower percentage of the new market value.

'With a currency, the yield is set by taking the key interest rate—say bank interest rates—as a percentage of the market value of the currency in US dollar terms. Now, if the Swiss franc is in strong international demand, as it usually is, its international price will be high and its yield low; that is to say that the interest rate you have to pay for borrowing the Swiss franc is low.

'But the very fact that the international market price for the Swiss franc is so high relative to, say, the Australian dollar means that any Australian who borrows Swiss francs and converts them into local currency is in constant danger of having the repayment value of his Swiss loan jump.

'For an Australian—a financially unskilled Australian, like your young farmer—to borrow Swiss francs on an uncovered basis is madness.'

After this conversation I did some scouting, and was appalled to find that in the early 1980s at least one substantial Australian trading bank had not only endorsed uncovered borrowing, but had also run seminars in provincial areas explaining the 'benefits' of uncovered Swiss franc borrowing. This was only possible on the part of the bank if its senior management—and presumably its board—were not merely ignorant of the dynamics of currency relationships, but ignorant as well of the dynamics of basic financial relationships. It beggared belief, but thousands of graziers, farmers, builders, developers, motel-chain operators, realtors, and other business figures had taken up the proposition underlying those seminars. It was difficult to know how many because most of them—people of substance in their towns and districts—were ashamed to show their faces: rather than expose their shame, most had absorbed the loss.

The Swiss franc loans debacle is one measure of how primitive the Australian financial system was as recently as 20 years ago. It demonstrates that, in the financial area at least, we had put ourselves at a disadvantage by becoming a self-governing nation. If banking in Australia had operated largely as branches of British establishments we would have been much less at risk. If our provincial managers had been trained at places like Tunbridge Wells and Leeds they would have known to box the ears of anyone coming to them with propositions to borrow uncovered Swiss francs for Australian finance.

We had four big banks at that point, which had grown up on Australia's ability to sell the world unprocessed wool and other raw materials and foods without getting involved in end products or the mysteries of international finance. Australian law gave these banks oligopoly status by protecting them against the entry of international competitors. The banks were able to operate like sultanates of the Ottoman Empire, sending their young men of promise out to the provinces as satraps with plenipotentiary status. Often a bank's judgement about a manager's suitability was based on how well they had married.

To understand what a gaffe the banks committed in endorsing uncovered Swiss-franc borrowing, it is necessary to understand recent Swiss history. The Swiss franc became the world's most desirable currency because the Swiss nation in the 20th century was a political eunuch. Instead of involving itself in the great events that preoccupied the rest of Europe, Switzerland concentrated on tending its garden—maintaining itself as a tidy, well-balanced place, cosseting large domestic savings, and incurring little debt. Such was its prudence and stability that in the 1970s Swiss banks were able to begin offering home mortgages to Swiss burghers equivalent to 100 per cent of the bank's valuation of their homes.

This was a very popular innovation. To fund the mortgages, the banks opened themselves to deposits from abroad. These arrived in droves, not because the interest rate on Swiss deposits was good—it was not—but because the prospect of Swiss currency up-valuation was constant. To keep in trim, the Swiss balanced long-term home lending domestically with short-term lending abroad. This was just about at the time when some Australian banks were enthusiastically encouraging their customers to incur exposure to Swiss finance in uncovered Australian-dollar terms.

The extreme danger of borrowing internationally in Swiss francs was not a temporary phenomenon. As a long-term trend, the value of the Swiss franc against major world currencies was upward: in 1915, one pound sterling was equal to 250 Swiss francs; by 2003, one pound sterling equalled 2.50 Swiss francs. Yet, for a decade in the latter part of the 20th century, benighted Australians who borrowed uncovered Swiss francs through their banks were encouraged by incredible banking incompetence to think that the only exchange rate which mattered between Switzerland and Australia was that which applied when the loan repayment was settled.

What foolishness. The Australian dollar stayed roughly in line with the pound sterling for most of the 20th century while, over the same period, broadly speaking, the Australian dollar depreciated against the Swiss franc by about 100 times its value. The fact that Australians—unlike the British—were simple enough to borrow in Swiss francs is a measure of how disastrously naïve and provincial our bankers had been for so long.

NEVERTHELESS, ONE SHOULDN'T PIN all of the blame for Australia's financial gaucherie on the banks. After Federation, we had woven for our financiers such a restrictive official cocoon that the banks could almost be excused their many faults. Our political leaders had evolved a bizarre regime for selling domestic government bonds in order to fund government deficits and, to support this regime, they had done two things. First, they had put bank deposit rates, bank lending rates, and savings bank mortgage rates under federal control to ensure that government bonds maintained their relative advantage to bank deposits. Then they ensured that life-insurance offices, pension funds, trading banks, savings banks, and other custodians of the people's savings had to keep a minimum of 20 per cent of their assets in the form of Commonwealth government bonds.

By these means, the government locked up the market for its own debt. To fund its debt, the federal government declared what it thought was a satisfactory price and yield for its bonds, and waited for the aforementioned institutions to turn up with the money. Given the arrangements constructed by the Commonwealth, it was a rare occurrence for it not to receive what it asked for.

Compare this with the great government bond market of New York. When I was in the United States, I watched with fascination the process of government bond-selling. The federal government would announce how much it needed to fund its deficit, and it would invite the investment houses to tender to deliver those funds. The investment houses would, in turn, set their best and brightest to the task of figuring out at what yield and price institutions would need to buy the bonds that were issued to cover the funds. This involved consideration of almost every aspect of modern life: the outlook for inflation, for politics, for international affairs, what the big developers were prepared to pay for money to build skyscrapers, and what the banks were prepared to pay for money to provide mortgages for homes.

The competing investment houses produced a variety of terms in prices and yields at which they would underwrite the federal government's bonds. When the government announced who had won the tender, there was an astonishing scramble in the victorious investment house. Breathless employees ran from the boardroom to seize the nearest phone and offload the new issue of bonds to life offices and pension funds. If there was trouble getting through, the emissaries of the underwriting house would jump in cabs and rush uptown to do the deals face to face. Every hour that passed cost the investment house money, for it had underwritten the government deficit with short-term borrowings. It was a wild, exciting race, as the firm sought to lay off the debt as quickly as it could in the long-term money market.

The American mode of government bond selling provided a front-line way of monitoring the economic system; it provided economic intelligence that the Australian system lacked. In the process of trying to establish the correct market price for the bond issue, the American investment houses and, by extension, the US federal government and Federal Reserve, very quickly learned if capital was starting to move out of government paper and into real assets — office blocks, condominiums, retirement developments in Florida, housing tracts. When this happened, it meant that the economy was starting to heat up, and the government accepted a tender bid at a higher interest rate. But if the intelligence coming in from the bids was that the long-term markets were starting to move from bricks and mortar back into government paper, the inclination was to accept a tender at the lower end of the range. The ease or the difficulty with which the investment houses placed the bond issue in the long-term market showed how correct the authorities' judgement had been.

In Australia, there was very little in the way of such early signals that the economy was turning from government paper to real assets and vice versa. Hence the economy tended to move in jerks. There would be an inflationary surge caught too late by the monetary authorities, or a slump similarly ill foreseen. Australia, too, had its bond investment houses, but the bond issue process here was nothing like the New York one. It didn't have to be. The Australian government had already decided the price and yield it would pay for its bonds, and although it had to wait to see how much of the market would accept those terms, there was little to worry about because the requirements to buy more or less forced the institutions' hands. The role of the Australian bond houses was largely to act as go-betweens: seeing what the savings banks thought about such-and-such a set of terms, seeing how they were placed as to 20 per cent requirements, and so on. It was a gentleman's profession; there was no undue rushing about.

The largest bond houses were in Melbourne, where the 'clubbiness' of the industry was reinforced by the closed culture of the investment houses. They reflected the narrowness of the city's establishment, which regarded even some of its own members with suspicion. Let me borrow here from the observations of Alan Reid, the late political journalist, who touched on the subject in his book *The Whitlam Venture* when considering the career of the conservative leader Malcolm Fraser, who brought down the Whitlam Labor government:

> From my scanty contact with the Victorian establishment, I formed the judgment that the establishment was, if not antagonistic, at least suspicious of Malcolm Fraser, clearly on what was put to me on several occasions, because they knew, or believed they knew, there was a Jewish forebear somewhere in Fraser's ancestry.
>
> Though this might seem an incredible basis for hostility to, or suspicion of, anyone, there does seem to be an anti-Semitic element in the Australian establishment, especially in Melbourne. Simon Warrender, a member of the staff of British Admiral Sir Charles Daniel, in charge of the British fleet fighting the Japanese in the Pacific with Australia as its base, writes: 'One evening after a meal at the Melbourne Club, I was asked to meet privately with one of the Club's leading members, a man who now holds a prominent position in Melbourne society ... He asked me, in a semi-secretive, almost conspiratorial, tone if it were true that Admiral Daniel was Jewish. 'The Admiral's name is Daniel I told him, and you only have to look at the man to realise he is not Scottish.'
>
> It was Club protocol, the man pointed out, a tacit agreement, that 'those people' were not admitted to the Melbourne Club. He asked me, quite seriously, to keep Admiral Daniel away from the Club as much as possible, or, if this could not be done to ensure discreetly that the Admiral stayed in the background and did not mix so freely with the members. (p 158)

In the early 1970s, I spent about a year in the investment industry in Melbourne after returning to Australia from the World Bank, and I can confirm the extraordinary prejudice encountered by Reid around that time. Quite charming gentlemen heading investment houses were adamant in their anti-Jewish prejudice. I asked a senior partner about this, and he explained that you could not take up a client relationship or an underwriting agreement with someone whom you could not take as a guest to the Melbourne Club.

These days, the role of the financial capital of Australia has moved from Melbourne to Sydney. And attitudes in the anti-Semitic Melbourne scene may well have changed. It is symbolic that J. B. Were and Son, the broking house once at the pinnacle of the Melbourne investment establishment, is now joined in marriage with the Wall Street investment house Goldman Sachs, under the name of Goldman Sachs J. B. Were, headquartered in Sydney. The founder of Goldman Sachs, late in the nineteenth century, was Marcus Goldman, a German–Jewish immigrant to the USA.

Nevertheless, the point remains valid: the insularity of the Australian financial world well into the 1980s, and the comparative openness of the American scene, demonstrated the fundamental social influences of different financial systems. In the US, when an investment house had won the competitive and risky right to underwrite an issue of government bonds, there was no room for prejudice on grounds of race or religion. It didn't matter whether the executive at the savings institution was Anglo-Saxon, Jewish, or Muslim. If he would take a large slice from you at a particular price and yield, he was your friend for life. Once a minority had become a force in American savings, there was no room for racial prejudice in the ruthlessly open and competitive world of finance. This is one reason why there is a disproportionately great Jewish influence on Wall Street. What matters most is hard competition.

But even the conservative culture of the Australian financial institutions does not fully explain how the Australian money market was able to continue to operate in a bubble. The variable that underpinned the nation's financial insularity for more than three-quarters of the twentieth century was the fixed rate of exchange for the Australian dollar. Our dollar—or pound, before 1966—was fixed first to sterling and then to the US dollar. In the latter part of its fixed regime it went through half-baked variations that didn't mean much. Fundamentally, it remained under the control of the federal government until early 1984. In this setting, it dictated the ebb and flow of both Australian economics and politics.

Its fixed value moved only under extreme pressure, according to the relativity of Australian inflation to the rest of the world, and the relativity of Australian export prices for wool, wheat, meat, metals, and minerals to the export prices of our trading partners. It may sometimes have moved according to the relationship between Australian unemployment and that of the rest of the world. The processes of its movements were dramatic: whenever Australian inflation would get out of line on the high side, the rest of the world, expecting the Australian government to have to devalue, would punt on the prospect by hauling more and more of their assets, short-term and long, outside Australia, until the breaking point came and they could come back in at a profit.

Alternatively, Australian wool prices would rise so steeply relative to imported goods that an up-valuation became obvious, and international punters would park short-term deposits in

Australian dollars until the break upward came and they could move back into their own currencies at a profit. These tugs-of-war jerked the Australian economy this way and that in a manner that lent a constant air of instability to the place.

Politically, the fixed exchange rate system provided an almost continuous air of excitement. The Australian countryman's perpetual line of economic expertise was the exchange rate: he always wanted it down, regardless of what was going on elsewhere, because the simple point was that by having it down he got more in Australian dollar terms for the goods he exported abroad. His focus on this transcended economics into a kind of spiritualism. The exchange rate was a spirit in a waterhole; to lay the spirit required acolytes to tend it, and priests to pray over it.

The leader of this religiosity was the Country Party, later renamed the National Party in the hope that people on the fringes of the cities might vote for it in numbers. At election times observance of the Country Party became intense: if the Country Party lifted its number of seats relative to its Coalition partner, the Liberal Party, the first assumption was that another devaluation of the Australian dollar was imminent. If the Country Party lost seats relatively, the exchange rate was probably firm for a while. This made political life particularly difficult for Malcolm Fraser, because he was a grazier torn between his perceived aristocratic responsibilities to the countryman and his responsibilities as prime minister of an urban nation.

In all, these and other factors set Australia up as a financially primitive nation in which new enterprise—aside from digging metals and minerals out of the ground and selling them abroad—became difficult. Our soldiers, opera singers, rock bands, and athletes were internationally celebrated, but the rest of us came to be regarded by the rest of the world as an unenterprising, feckless lot. We were frequently warned by neighbours such as Lee Kuan Yew, prime minister of Singapore, and Mahathir Mohamad, prime minister of Malaysia, that unless we lifted our game we would be swamped by an advancing Asia. Indeed, it was Lee Kuan Yew who first told us, in a not unfriendly way, that we were in danger of becoming 'the white trash of Asia'.

Australia's second-rate economic status was the result of a constricted, insular financial system, and a banking system that was constipated, incompetent, over-cautious, arrogant, and shallow. The highlight of the year for the big Australian banks was to send their chairmen and managing directors to the World Bank and International Monetary Fund annual meetings. These two institutions held their annual meetings alternately at their home base of Washington and a site elsewhere in the world. Like a band of boarding-school boys going on an outing, the heads of the Australian banks would gather together and set out for Washington or some destination even more exotic.

(While I was at the World Bank the authorities there decided that they would hold their next meeting in the southern hemisphere. Australia was proposed, but which city? Why, Melbourne, of course. When my small voice made the point that the Reserve Bank of Australia had recently established its headquarters in Sydney, the authorities looked at me in some surprise. Ultimately, the hedonists won the day: they chose Rio de Janeiro instead.)

The Australians had no intention of contributing to the order of business—they would not have known how to—but knew they would meet important people at morning and afternoon tea, and in the evenings they and their wives could expect to be regularly engaged in the cocktail parties of at least the Anglo-Saxon countries and the old British Empire countries like India, Pakistan, and Sri Lanka, and perhaps places like Saudi Arabia and Bahrain who were often looking for people.

Usually, the Australians were of little interest to others, and kept to their own small set on the fringe. Sometimes, if there was a mining boom in Australia, they attracted broader attention. In fact, those conversations at cocktail parties at the Washington Hilton, the Washington Sheraton, and the Bahrain Embassy during the height of the Australian mining boom of the late 1960s sowed the seed of the financial revolution that would transform Australia. The Australian bankers were thrilled when their New York or London counterparts walked up to them and said, 'I'm beginning to hear a lot about what's happening out there. Minerals and metals, you've got 'em, boys. We must do something together.'

The Australians failed to explain that Australian law prevented 'doing something together' if that entailed another licensed bank in this country; or, indeed, that they were happy with their closed shop, and that the last thing they wanted was another Australian licensed bank in their midst. So it proved embarrassing when some of these great and powerful international banks sought to follow through and then discovered that they were not allowed to.

To mollify the deflated internationals, the Australian banks proposed, 'Let's start something together outside the licensing system; something like a merchant bank.' Setting up a merchant bank (or an investment bank, as the Americans call it), involves assembling a collection of bright young people capable of launching successful businesses with other people's money.

There followed a series of announcements of new merchant bank and investment bank start-ups involving an Australian bank and one, or perhaps two, foreign banks.

It was not the formation of these 'joint ventures' that sparked the Australian financial revolution; it was what happened soon after. The joint ventures themselves were largely failures: the mining boom crashed in the wake of the first great oil squeeze; and when the new ventures turned to financing a property boom, the Whitlam government saw to it that that crashed, too. (A bond market collapse associated with Whitlam's political and economic crisis did for the property boom.) By the mid-1970s, these joint ventures were making losses, some at or near the value of paid-up capital. The international banks quietly went away.

However, in order to fill their part of the original joint-venture deals, the Australian banks had had to hastily scrape together the 'collection of bright young people' that had been part of the deal. Having not much to contribute from the banks' own ranks, this talent was recruited overseas among young Australians graduating or recently graduated from the Harvard Business School, the Massachusetts Institute of Technology and so on, as well as similarly educated young people in broking houses and investment companies. When the joint ventures failed or faded, disappointment ran through the ranks of these financially bright, well-educated young Australians who had returned home.

DISSATISFACTION WITH THE STATUS QUO in Australia's financial structure and climate became a political force among the talented young in Sydney, finding its voice most effectively through an economist and political activist called John Hewson. Hewson had observed Australian financial insularity and inefficiency during his posting with the IMF in Washington. The more he learned about the American and the international financial systems, the more appalled he became with what he saw in Australia.

He returned to Australia in 1975 on nothing less than a crusade to free the system from within its political superstructure. His landing point was as an economist with the Reserve Bank of Australia, but the RBA found him a bit much, and within a year he was ensconced as an economic advisor to Phillip Lynch, then treasurer in the Fraser government. Hewson had the hopes of the disaffected riding with him as he set about using his position to overhaul financial legislation and regulation. He and dozens of others in the upmarket bars and coffee shops of Sydney saw this as the way to free Australia of its shackles.

John Howard replaced the ailing Lynch as treasurer, becoming Hewson's boss. By this time, Hewson had decided that the way to reform the Australian financial system was to put together a committee to inquire into every aspect of Australian finance, and to use this to overturn the old regime. Thus began a power struggle between John Hewson, on the one side, and political, bureaucratic, and business muscle on the other. It took Hewson four years to get his committee up and running, and it would prove to be the most important independent committee of inquiry in the Australian federation's history. But for such a high-profile body, its membership and its list of back-up advisors and commissioned contributors was scrappy.

The chairman, Keith Campbell, was a very able man but, as chairman and managing director of L. J. Hooker, he did not come from an establishment institution. His deputy, Alan Coates, who was general manager of AMP, did, but Coates was a one-off: broadminded, open to new ideas, a man ahead of his time at AMP. And though he supported the committee's aims, he thought it prudent to be number two rather than number one. Keith Halkerston, another member of the committee, was a very smart independent in the financial scene, in the process of making a fortune in conjunction with a new merchant bank called Hill Samuel; but he was, by personality, a brilliant loner. Next came Dick McCrossin, general manager of a fringe institution called the Australian Resources Development Bank. Then there was Jim Mallyon, from the RBA, there to project and protect the Reserve Bank's burgeoning position in the official financial family; and, finally, there was the committee's secretary, Fred Argy, a refugee from Commonwealth Treasury who had sought the haven of a Macquarie University posting.

The committee's list of advisors and commissioned contributors was just as interesting. Representation from the 'four pillars' banks was notable by its absence. The only Commonwealth Treasury representative on the list was the tough-minded individualist Ted Evans, later head of the Treasury under Paul Keating. The banks on the list were foreign institutions such as Citibank, Hong Kong and Shanghai, Bank of Tokyo, Bank of America, and Barclays Bank. The ace from outside was the economist and Nobel laureate Professor Milton Friedman of Chicago. It was clear that the Australian banks and, to some extent, the business establishment generally, were shunning the exercise. On one occasion, Howard, returning to Canberra from Sydney, informed Hewson that Bob White, the head of Westpac, 'doesn't think the Campbell inquiry is such a good idea'.

That must have come close to sounding the death knell of the Campbell Committee of Inquiry; if nothing else, it was a warning that the most important of the committee's recommendations would be knee-capped. The fact that the report was finished and tabled in parliament was a tribute to the doggedness, drive, and tenacity of John Hewson. Its survival was his most important political achievement, but he could not have foreseen the political circumstances that would bring an economic revolution to life.

Chapter 2

The Revolution Begins

'Don't you know each cloud contains pennies from heaven?' –Johnny Mercer

CLOUDS IN DEEP BANKS HUNG OVER THE PROGRESS OF THE Campbell Committee of Enquiry's report into the Australian financial system. The Fraser government tabled the report in the House of Representatives in November 1981. By the time Labor defeated Fraser in 1983, some reforms, including the establishment of a bond tender system, had crept through. But key recommendations of the committee, including the floating of the dollar and the removal of exchange controls, had remained untouched.

In some ways, it was surprising that anything at all went through under Fraser. When the report was submitted, someone directed the prime minister's attention to a consultant's analysis of the housing-finance component, contained in an appendix. The consultant had declared, erroneously, that housing interest rates would rise by two percentage points if they were deregulated. Fraser's initial response to the Campbell Committee's report was therefore to go straight to the appendix, find the offending material, and then pitch the document across the table, saying, 'That's that, then.'

John Hewson, who witnessed this, rushed down the corridor to John Howard's office. 'You can't let him do this,' the young advisor urged Howard. 'The markets have been full of what will flow from this report for months now. Expectations have been raised. You will look bloody stupid if you allow this just to be shelved.'

'But what can we do?' Howard said. 'Malcolm definitely does not want to do it.' Both sat for a time staring out the window and at the ceiling.

At length, Hewson suggested, 'Look, let's set up a taskforce to bring before cabinet recommendations based on the report, in a sequence that you can control. You will kill yourself politically if you allow the thing to be jettisoned. Shelving it will be seen as just a short-term populist thing, and you will go down in history as the person responsible for its shelving.'

Howard concurred and, by degrees, papers from the taskforce began to go to cabinet. Today there is still debate about who drove the reforms and about how far they went. One line holds that Malcolm Fraser squandered eight years of precious power and did nothing; another argues that without Malcolm Fraser there would have been no financial deregulation, and that Fraser's contribution on this front has been unjustly unrecognised. A third, proposed by the Howard camp, was that Howard was blocked from delivering vigorous economic and financial reform by the hidebound combination of Malcolm Fraser and the Country Party. If that is true, I have to ask: where are the cabinet submissions that Howard lost out on?

It appears that Howard, without the continuous urging and pushing of his advisor, would have been disinclined to stand up to Fraser on the Campbell recommendations. The few that were enacted before the election would not have made it without Hewson.

But Howard has enjoyed a charmed life when it comes to the historical record of his tenure as treasurer. While failing to give Hewson the backing he so needed for the Campbell report and its recommendations, he simultaneously presided over an economic mess. Business interest rates reached 21 per cent, but to no avail in terms of economic governance. In 1981, wages grew by 16 per cent, leading to a recession marked by a combination of stagnant growth and high inflation. By the time Howard handed over the economy to Labor in 1983, the economy was growing at only 1.4 per cent, the unemployment rate was 11 per cent, and inflation had reached 11 per cent. Paul Keating's comment years later was fair enough: 'We went into Howard's recession with double-digit inflation and we came out with double-digit inflation. Whereas, from my time, in the so-called recession we had to have, we went into it with inflation at about 7 per cent and we came out with it at 1 per cent. And, as a consequence, we had the decade of the 1990s and beyond with continuous low inflationary growth.'

Hewson's contribution as Howard's advisor has been under-recognised but, happily for him, he is not a man in need of psychological nurturing. He still believes that the huge financial reform was largely his own work: that it was the establishment of his 'parameters' that allowed the dollar to be floated at the end of 1983, the year Labor was elected. Says Hewson, 'I had already gone to the people who ran the wool exchange and there we got a currency futures exchange going and a forward market for the dollar. Once a significant external crisis came along, a float of the currency was inevitable.'

I don't agree with John Hewson about this inevitability. In this matter, Malcolm Fraser's heart was with the National Party. Had the Fraser government been re-elected in 1983, politics would have governed the future of the dollar. The National Party would have demanded a stop to all the nonsense of freeing the dollar—especially given that, when the 'external crisis' came along, it was towards an up-valuation of the currency rather than the devaluation which the National Party would have wanted. Fraser would have been keen to stop the floating of the dollar at this point, and Treasury would have supported him. John Stone and other senior officials in Treasury opposed the float and, as far as they were concerned, the less they saw of John Hewson the better.

It took Labor to float the dollar. The float was central to the Campbell reforms; without it, history would have turned out very differently. For one thing, Macquarie Bank could not have emerged as it did from the Hill Samuel investment house.

BLUE-SKY OPTIMISM PREVAILED at Hill Samuel Australia as the political parties prepared for the 1983 election. Fraser and Howard would win the election, they believed, and progress on the Campbell recommendations would pick up to the point of allowing the growth that the young HSA team had been conditioned to expect. As things turned out, they were a lot luckier than they could know.

Political luck produced the Macquarie Bank. But the bank did not emerge perfectly formed, a sort of financial Venus rising from the waves. There were 16 years of gestation, led by a young man named David Clarke, who was not unlike John Hewson in his determination and drive to create something new in Australia. His passions were rugby, opera, bridge, wine, philately, gold and, accountancy, and his creative genius lay outside politics, except to the extent that he helped create a solid base for John Howard in New South Wales.

It was in 1971 that Clarke first got together with his original partners, Mark Johnson and Tony Berg, to form the enterprise that started the Macquarie Group adventure. Clarke and Berg had both attended Knox Grammar, and all three had studied at Harvard University. Now they found themselves together again, at the Sydney investment bank Darling and Company. Not far away, down the hill towards Circular Quay, a young Englishman had established a small enterprise called Hill Samuel Australia as an outpost of the substantial British bank Hill Samuel London. The Englishman was impatient with his Australian sojourn, and wanted to get back to the action in London. So, one sparkling day on Sydney harbour, aboard Mark Johnson's yacht, he asked Clarke and Johnson if they would consider taking over his task of building up Hill Samuel in Australia. They had not been not very impressed with the pace of Darling and Company, so they soon agreed, and Berg joined them.

The three worked well together, and they began to succeed in conventional merchant banking—mergers and acquisitions, and using other people's money to kick-start successful businesses. Clarke was a good accountant and a brilliant organiser, and what helped them through their early days when other merchant banks and investment banks were disappearing, was a system of organisation not unlike that of the Soviet Communist Party, where one cadre shadowed another on assignment. Hill Samuel pitched aggressively for business, but ranging beside the loan salesman it always had a risk manager whose job it was to check and re-check the client's credit-worthiness before the loan was given. In the early days of the operation, Clarke set the example by doing a fair amount of the checking and re-checking himself.

This system stood them in good stead through the crisis atmosphere that prevailed in Australia's financial world in the wake of the mining-boom bust and the Whitlam years. Hill Samuel stayed largely free of problem loans, and was able to pick up bargain-basement deals in these first fifteen years. The bank prospered, and its flat management structure, employees' reward plans, and an environment that encouraged people with new ideas to develop them, began to make it the envy of other young financiers who had been less well-served by the traditional banks.

But an enterprise doesn't achieve the momentum of Hill Samuel simply by good staff management and a special risk-management structure alone. It also needs a capacity to innovate that is akin to business genius. The organisation first manifested this when David Clarke and Keith Halkerston, the boutique financier who served on the Campbell Committee, talked through an idea that Halkerston had for a cash-management enterprise.

Its basis was the gap that existed between the interest rate that Australia's licensed commercial banks paid their depositors and the interest returns that the same banks derived by investing the depositors' money in the increasing array of professional money-market paper, open only to large operators. In this market, gilt-edged paper circulated, ranging from Commonwealth Treasury notes to bank-guaranteed commercial bills. In the turbulent times of the 1970s and 1980s, their yields could go above 20 per cent for extended periods.

By comparison, the returns available to individual bank depositors were petty. One needed to have a minimum cache well above the capacity of most individual investors to play in the professional discounted bills and notes market.

Hill Samuel set up a trust which worked in the following way: those dissatisfied with the returns they could get as bank depositors were gathered together to pool their money in a Hill Samuel trust that took the pooled funds into the professional money-market, where they were invested in discounted notes and bills, all of blue-chip status. The Hill Samuel trust then paid out to its members interest-rate returns almost as high as those prevailing in the professional money-market, and far above the rates they could have got as bank depositors. It was a simple idea, but it needed boldness, judgement, and drive to carry it through successfully.

The Hill Samuel Cash Management Trust took off like wildfire. Within four months it attracted $100 million from erstwhile bank depositors. In time, deposits in the trust grew to $1 billion and went on from there. With hindsight, it is evidence that the elements that have made Macquarie Group one of the most successful financial enterprises in the world were already in place. First, the infant Hill Samuel seized on the existence of high and often government-guaranteed yields that would be available to investors only through the medium of an organisation with boldness and esprit de corps. Then it moved to mortgages: it realised that between the cost of deposits to banks and the income they received from mortgage payments made by Australian home-buyers was another substantial gap—a gold mine for the licensed banks.

It became clear to the people at Hill Samuel that if you bundled individual home mortgages together into packages of, say, 1000; and if, as you did so, you insured each mortgage with the entity that the Commonwealth government had recently established—the Home Loans Insurance Corporation—you were, to all intents and purposes, creating a new gilt-edged security. Between the savings interest rates that the four-pillars banks paid on deposits and the interest they received on home mortgages there was a gap in which the saver could be rewarded substantially with higher rates, and the home mortgagor rewarded with lower rates.

First, though, Hill Samuel needed new organisations for creating mortgages at the grass roots. So they went downtown, beyond the portals of the big banks' saving branches, and chummed up with brokers such as John Symond, now well known as the founder of Aussie Home Loans. The broker would collect batches of home mortgages, and Hill Samuel would rush these bundles to the Home Loans Insurance Corporation to have them processed while at the same time putting some of its own funds at risk briefly by paying the broker some $50 million with which to go out and create a fresh harvest of home loans.

Hill Samuel then presented its bundles of sanitised, fully insured home mortgages to superannuation funds and other institutions starving for something more rewarding in yield than the Commonwealth bonds and semi-governmental bonds for state electricity, water, and so on, to which they were largely confined. On the way through, the prices of the mortgage bonds rose as they became gilt-edged. The loans left the broker priced to yield, say, 8 per cent; by the time they were presented to the pension funds and life offices, the 'securitised' mortgage bundles would be priced to yield, say, 7 per cent, implying a profit to Hill Samuel on the way through. And why not? In the large gap between the big banks' savings deposit rate and their mortgage rate, there was room for the brokers to run a good business providing mortgages below the banks' mortgage rate, room for Hill Samuel to make a profit, and room for the pension funds to get a gilt-edged yield better than they could anywhere else.

The pension funds and the life offices had the task of providing for retirees outside the public service and the meagre benefits of the government's aged pension. As the numbers of aged Australians rose, this responsibility became more onerous because of the limited return on government paper. The arrival of the Hill Samuel mortgage-bond yields was at first a welcome extra, but soon became indispensable as the supply of these mortgage bonds swelled. Indeed, as the years passed, the supply of securities created by Hill Samuel and then the Macquarie Bank completely reversed the outlook for these savings institutions, allowing them to pump more and more in pension funds out to the savers of Australia.

Hill Samuel, and then Macquarie, also reversed the outlook for the Australian household-assets market. Because of their increased affordability, the demand for homes rose through the 1980s and 1990s. A permanent shift in demand occurred, and with that came a permanent shift upward in the value of ordinary people's homes. It was not a shift that occurred at the expense of other asset markets such as the share market because it was a value occurring through an increase in the velocity of money circulating in the economy. The laziness of money flows allowed by the yawning gap between bank deposit rates and bank lending rates was gone forever.

Between developing Hill Samuel and becoming the Macquarie Bank, David Clarke and his colleagues worked at being the most creative and profitable financial entrepreneurs in this country. They knew that if they kept going at this pace they would have to spread their wings worldwide. They needed to be able to trade Australian dollars in the key markets of the world and to shift funds in and out of Australia without hindrance. As they saw it, they would have this opportunity when John Hewson, with the backing of John Howard, got the external components of his Campbell bundle through the new Fraser government in 1983. In the meantime, as if in training for the wider opportunities that would supposedly flow from the Hewson–Howard–Fraser combination, young people from Hill Samuel were beginning to go around the world 'constantly willing to learn', as David Clarke put it to me in an early interview. 'Actually, they find they don't encounter much that they don't already know. We are constantly investing in that sort of knowledge.'

The big success of the mortgage bonds and the cash-management trust gave David Clarke the cash flow he needed to build his staff and attend to their education. Each year he went to the top management schools of North America seeking outstanding Australians and New Zealanders looking for something to come home to. Later, other executive directors joined Clarke on this annual drive, but at first he made the circuit alone. Young Hill Samuel people went on to look for connections in Tokyo, Hong Kong, and Singapore, as well as using their parental connection in London.

Australia's junior status among the nations turned out to be an advantage at key points. In Australia, Hill Samuel staff had developed an expert capacity in trading a wide range of derivatives, in everything from gold to shares. The basis for derivatives trading is the selling and buying of an option: to supply or to take a security or an asset like gold at a certain price at a certain time. You can make this as simple or as complicated as you like, and in the Australian trade the Hill Samuel people honed their skills right along the ladder of possibilities. When they went to Tokyo, they discovered that the Tokyo market, though it was the third-largest securities market in the world, knew next to nothing about derivatives trading. The Japanese were anxious to learn a great deal more, but they feared loss of face in approaching New York or London for tuition.

Thus they welcomed the arrival of these Australians who knew just about all there was to know about derivatives trading. There would be no loss of face involved in setting up some joint front, behind which furious tuition could occur. Thus Hill Samuel formed a 'joint venture' with the Industrial Bank of Japan to teach the Japanese all about derivatives trading, and the link proved invaluable in later years as Macquarie became active around the world.

Hill Samuel met varying degrees of sophistication in different places. Hong Kong at that time was more developed and sophisticated because it had had a period of freedom to do what it liked, more or less; Britain had accepted the demise of its colonial status, and Communist China had not yet moved in. Such settings tend to give rise to a desperate creativity, as with art and theatre in Weimar Germany, and trade and sex in pre-war Shanghai. Hong Kong in the interregnum between British and Chinese control was a place full of talented traders ready to try anything in securities skills in a free market, and Hill Samuel people were ready to mix it with the best of them. Macquarie subsequently established its own operation in Hong Kong.

For Hill Samuel London, its investment in the Australian

bank spectacularly outshone initial expectations. Relations between the Clarke team and the parent company remained amicable through to the end, but the Australian operation did not adopt the culture of its London parent. Under its parent's culture, Hill Samuel Australia would have gone to Hong Kong because the managing director considered, for some reason or other, that they should be there. Hill Samuel London opened an office in New York which never made any money, but which nevertheless could be charged off against other parts of the organisation.

Neither Hill Samuel Australia nor Macquarie would work that way, there were (and still are) no offices abroad that did not thoroughly justify themselves as centres of profitable business. So, from the start, the Australian operation built a culture of its own. This difference meant that its Australian principals regarded it as imperative that, when Australia's banking laws and currency regulations opened up sufficiently, Hill Samuel Australia should have a plan in place to enable the investment house to become an independent Australian entity.

By the early 1980s, David Clarke and the Hill Samuel Australia hierarchy were determined to separate from their London parent, for they were chafing under their parent's authority and there was an increasing cultural gulf between London and Sydney. The Australian hierarchy felt that the existing structure could lead to destructive friction if it was left in place.

While Hill Samuel Australia waited to see who would be in power after the 1983 elections, David Clarke and his colleagues informally assessed the task ahead of them. If things went well and the dollar was floated and currency restrictions were removed, the rationale for establishing their own enterprise, Macquarie Bank, would be complete. This would mean changing from 100 per cent foreign ownership to being no more than 15 per cent foreign-owned. Given the great value that Clarke and the team had managed to build into Hill Samuel Australia in 12 years, this would mean a big capital challenge. To buy 85 per cent of the parent company's stake immediately would be too great a task. With friends like John Hewson and John Howard reinforced in power, however, they reasoned that it should be possible to get the full 85 per cent ownership delayed; perhaps a 70 per cent buy-down first, and the remaining 15 per cent requirement some time later. Even that would be hard sledding, but they thought they could manage it once the Fraser government was re-elected.

The staff wanted the greatest share of any new bank that they could manage to pay for, and this could be assisted if the staff cashed in their equity profit-share and option entitlements. This could give them all about 15 per cent. But this would still leave more than 50 per cent of the capital to be found. A deal with existing Australian banks was clearly out of the question: they were still seething over the hundreds of millions of dollars that Hill Samuel were taking from them in their cash-management trust and mortgage-bond innovations. But, aside from this, having one or more local banks participate in the new entity would mean swapping one form of stultification for another that was even worse.

So Hill Samuel Australia decided they'd have to go to pension funds and life office institutions—the people they had served well with extra income—and ask them to take an equity interest in any new bank. To get that to about 55 per cent of the capital would require hard sums, hard talk, and hard slog. It would be a tough job to hold their nerve well enough to bed the new bank down, without compromising their principles.

THUS, for the Hill Samuel Australia team, the 1983 election approached with a great deal riding on it. Fraser was favoured to win over Bill Hayden, leader of the opposition. But it would be no walkover. The Fraser government was finishing its term without glowing economic credentials: the budget deficit for the 1983–84 year was estimated at above $8 billion, interest rates were high, and inflation was running at 11 per cent. The one big thing the coalition had going for it was the electorate's collective memory of near-anarchy under the Whitlam government.

From the future Macquarie team the salute to Fraser's coalition team was 'May the force be with you.' The story of the 1983 election must surely begin with Malcolm Fraser's desire to become a good golfer. His wife, Tammie, was good at golf, and it was one of Fraser's lifetime disappointments that he could not match her. It was not a matter of marital rivalry; he was a bigger man than that. It was rather that on overseas visits—particularly Asian visits—the prime minister repeatedly found himself having to explain that, although they had grown up in the same social stratum with much the same social activities, he was not the golfer his wife was. The disparity suggested that in his youth he had been a nerdy swat.

Fraser found a professional golfer, Neville Wilson, at a course in Belconnen, a good distance from both Parliament House and Royal Canberra Golf Club. Whenever he got a spare hour, he would have his driver whiz him out there so that he and the pro could work on the PM's game. As with many talented, driven men, Fraser let golf become an obsession for a time. He would hit dozens of buckets of balls over a few weeks, and soon a mere bucket at a time became insufficient: he moved to garbage cans half-filled with balls. He had an almighty but erratic swing, and on the occasions when the swing connected he would send the ball beyond the driving range into houses across the road.

Unless they are in their youth, golfers who persist too much on the practice range are likely to suffer for it. This is what happened to Fraser: he persisted so much that he put his back out badly. His doctors prescribed sustained rest in a prone position. For a man of action like Fraser, this was quite unfamiliar; and the longer the enforced rest went on, the more time he had to mull over problems. Lying there, political strategies began to whirl in his brain.

Bob Hawke had recently resigned as president of the Australian Council of Trade Unions to become a Labor Party backbencher, as a preliminary move to becoming leader of the federal opposition, and then, as he saw it, prime minister. Fraser, from his hospital bed, began to see two reasons for calling an early election. He was shrewd enough to see Hawke's political appeal to Australians—his larrikin persona and his audacious, combative flow of words. It would not be a good idea to give Hawke enough time to take leadership of the party.

At the same time, Hawke had been on the backbench long enough to begin some scratching of the ground around Bill Hayden. Reports coming to Malcolm Fraser were that these had initiated stirrings of instability in a party that was, until then, firmly behind their leader. Hayden had the prestige of being one of the few members of the Whitlam cabinet to have emerged with his reputation unscathed from Labor's time in office. The parliamentary Labor Party, shocked and frightened at the destruction of the Whitlam government, was grateful for a man of status and substance to rally around. That was Hayden. On the other hand, there was Bob Hawke, a natural politician and leader. They began to think it was a pity that Hawke had not been there earlier.

Fraser could see that the timing of the election would be crucial in these circumstances. The earlier the better, he decided, so he set an election date for early 1983, months before the poll was due. To his amazement, Hayden countered—within 20 minutes of Fraser making his election call public—by resigning from the leadership of his party in favour of Bob Hawke. It was the sweetest of bloodless coups. Hayden was later to offer the view that a drover's dog could have led Labor to victory in 1983.

Whatever the reasoning behind Bill Hayden's move, Malcolm Fraser was trumped. Hayden, a patently decent man with a good economic brain and reputation, might have won against a Fraser–Howard combination. But, again, he might not have. The dramatic elevation of Hawke put a Labor victory beyond doubt. To jump suddenly from leader of the trade unions to prime ministerial candidate for the Labor Party was a leap of daring that Douglas Fairbanks might have admired, and it suited Hawke's personality. He was able to sweep aside fears left over from the Whitlam era; he was going to quell inflation and union instability via various wage-and-price constraining schemes.

Hawke's team won in a landslide. To the financial community, this was a shock. Certainly, Hawke and Keating had promised a reformist government, but would they really carry through the recommendations of the Campbell report? The committee's terms of reference said it was to assess the importance of the efficiency of the Australian financial system 'for the government's free enterprise objectives'. Were 'free enterprise objectives' a major concern for this Labor government? Were they even welcome to a Labor government? Since the internal split in the Labor Party in the 1950s, the Left had re-emerged.

Immediately after the Hawke government's election in March 1983, the prospect of 'free enterprise' financial policies must have appeared bleak: three days after that election the new government devalued the Australian dollar by 10 per cent. This formal change in the currency by fiat was the antithesis of what David Clarke's team needed for its great leap forward. Anyone within the bank with a close knowledge of recent Labor Party history must have despaired at this initial act. Aside from Hawke and Keating—a couple of hard-edged pragmatists not over-burdened with dogma—the core of the party, the Labor caucus, was best viewed as an entity quite disinclined to 'free enterprise'.

The nature of the caucus is best illustrated by their reverence for the soul of a man who had gone from them too soon. Eddie Ward, the federal Labor member for East Sydney, erstwhile tramway linesman and professional boxer, was (and still is) loved by Labor's true believers for his principles and his rapier-like ability to pierce 'the Tories' in debate. Throughout Sir Robert Gordon Menzies' glory days in the 1950s and 1960s, Ward was the only one to get under Menzies' skin, with allegations about Menzies' affair with a Fairfax maiden and, more importantly, Menzies complicity in what Labor called the 'the Brisbane line' plot. This was a supposed secret policy to abandon Australia to the Japanese, north of a line running through Brisbane. The former pugilist endeared himself most to the true believers with his rough wit: Menzies' burgeoning military career, said Ward, had been cut short by the outbreak of World War I.

Eddie Ward had served in parliament since 1931. When I joined the Canberra Press Gallery in the mid-1950s, I felt it my business to introduce myself to Ward soon after my arrival there. We chatted across the Magna Carta case in King's Hall in the old Parliament House, in the course of which Eddie outlined the principal planks of his political philosophy: the World Bank and the International Monetary Fund were front institutions set up to support American capitalist power, and Australia should withdraw from them. He believed that under American capitalist power we were heading for 'a dictatorship of New York robber barons which would be just as terrible as any of the Hitlerite dreams'. The New York robber baron program would remove decent employment for people like us; 'slavery, degradation, financial destruction' were what we faced under American domination.

A government under 'someone like myself or Clyde Cameron,' Eddie stated, would remove private finance from Australia. We would have the banks in the public sector. We would have stringent central planning as the basis for this economy. We would have a foreign policy completely independent of America. The policy of Eddie Ward would see 'the little man protected by socialisation, union power, central social welfare and full employment'. It was an anachronistic ideology that highlighted Labor's socialist origins but, even in the 1960s, it still had plenty of supporters among party members and in the broader electorate.

Ward stood for election to deputy leader of the party in 1960 and was narrowly defeated by Gough Whitlam. When, under the leadership of Arthur Calwell, Labor lost a recession election in 1961, the left urged Ward to stand as leader, indicating its increased strength after the election. But by then Eddie Ward was nearing his end. He died of heart disease in 1963 and, as time went on, he became a Labor saint. His mantle passed to a charismatic younger leader of the left, Jim Cairns, who continued to advocate collective ownership of industry and opposition to the corrosive influence of capitalism. Cairns and, from Sydney, another member of the left faction, Tom Uren, were stars of the federal Labor parliamentary party; meanwhile, the left was resurgent in union politics, among both the rank and file and the leadership.

Whitlam twice defeated Cairns in ballots for the Labor leadership; his modernising vision for the party prevailed, including his plans to slash trade tariffs and introduce wage indexation. Yet, at the time the Hawke government was elected in 1983, a significant core of Labor remained atavistically opposed to free-market politics. From the party's adoption of its socialisation objective in 1921 to the collectivism of Jim Cairns and the New Left, layer upon layer of anti-capitalism had accreted in the sediment of the ALP's soul. In this unpromising environment, the continued existence of Hill Samuel appeared difficult enough; that the bank would not only survive but flourish under a Labor government must have seemed an impossibility.

Yet under the Hawke–Keating government, Clarke and his team were to receive all the 'free enterprise' structure they needed. Hill Samuel Australia was to become the fully licensed Macquarie Group, freed from the deadening regulation that had hung over the Australian financial sector, and equipped with the necessary powers to be an international capitalist player. It was also to benefit greatly from the rush towards the workers' superannuation schemes that treasurer Keating instituted—above all else, new financial capital was what Macquarie needed to grow. Of course, compulsory workplace superannuation was not a beneficent measure designed for Macquarie Group by the ALP, but this was to be its impact. Its effect would be to turbo-charge the Australian securities market with new capital. The flow of capital from workers' pensions into the markets was to convert the Sydney capital market into one of the most liquid and most powerfully growing in the world, worth $1 trillion by 2006.

Underpinning all this was a free-flowing and flexible economy, and fundamental to it was the floating of the Australian dollar. The background to the float is a story of tension and exceptional opportunity for policy change. Upon gaining power as treasurer, Paul Keating rapidly organised a slap-up financial committee of enquiry to review the conclusions of the Campbell Committee. It was a political ploy, but it was accepted by the business and financial establishment. Wisely, the government appointed as its head a private-sector banker of the old school, Vic Martin, who was at the time executive chairman of MLC. The Martin Committee's job, in effect, was to review the conclusions of the Campbell Committee quick-smart—and, if possible, to give them a stamp of approval.

As 1983 progressed, the Martin Committee began to attract international attention. Was the ALP really going to do it? The international financial community saluted Labor by pouring money into the Australian capital account. If they hadn't liked what they saw, they would have swiftly pulled it out again. But, more and more, they felt optimistic about the Australian economy under Hawke Labor, and they sent money in until the 'net' in net capital inflow began to loom large.

This was a mixed blessing for Labor's leaders. Certainly, they liked the vote of approval from abroad. But their first job in domestic management was to bring the inflation they had inherited under control, and in particular to bring a wages push under control. With its currency still fixed in the latter part of 1983, the money coming from abroad was going into Australia's domestic money base; with a floating currency, it would have pushed the currency up externally, leaving domestic money unaltered. But by the second half of the year, domestic money-supply growth was running at 15 per cent, an ominous hazard for controlling a wages push: if they simply let that continue, Hawke Labor could have quickly reverted to the early situation under Whitlam Labor.

The money and currency prospect for Australia became a race between the Martin Committee's ability to quickly produce its report with recommendations providing an objective basis for releasing the Australian dollar and the accelerating determination of international funds managers to make a killing out of the new enthusiasm for Australia under Labor. The currency was now under full-blooded speculative pressure. In the last four months of 1983, a net $4 billion flowed from abroad into the Australian money base. In the first nine days of December, $1.5 billion flowed in. The breaking point was rushing up just as the Martin Committee was preparing to report. Paul Keating grabbed the favourable conclusion on floating the dollar from the text of the committee's report as soon as he saw it, and made it law on the night of 9 December. It was the boldest, most profound, reform by a treasurer in the relatively brief history of Australia. Said Keating: 'Speculators can now speculate against themselves and not against the Australian government.'

And speculators did speculate among themselves at that initial break point, to the extent of driving the Australian dollar to a peak of 97 US cents. It soon emerged that there was going to be a deep international inter-bank trading market for the Australian currency which, facilitated by the removal of the residual constraints and regulations pertaining to the fixed regime, would allow the steady development of an orderly market in the currency. This the nascent Macquarie Group could view with pleased anticipation and timely preparation.

All this happened via the skilful use of committees and, at the top end of the Hawke government, through a couple of political leaders with the instincts of poker players. But to understand the thrilling sweep of it all through that year, one must understand the singular nature of one man in particular.

Chapter 3

The Blooding of Paul Keating

'The legend was that visitors to Donnybrook Fair would rather fight than eat.' –Michael Quinion

BY THE TIME HE WAS 24, PAUL KEATING HAD ENDURED A MORE intense physical and psychological blooding in politics than most budding MPs would experience in a decade.

His career was born in the long years of turmoil that followed the Split in the Labor Party. It was Herbert Vere Evatt, then leader of the federal parliamentary party, who precipitated the Split in October 1954, by accusing right-wing Catholics in the ALP of treachery. As a result, he not only broke the anti-communist adventure in Australian Labor; he opened the gates of parliamentary Labor and the unions once again to the disciples of Eddie Ward. Back into the party came a stream of crypto-communist, anti-capitalist, popular-front romantics, who got their first chance to show their capacity for real damage when they became the core of caucus in the disastrous Whitlam government.

Their successors are still out there in the parliamentary party and in left-wing union executives, waiting for their next opportunity to turn the clock back to state pensions and other nanny-state measures. They are the real Australian conservatives, not in the capitalist sense but in the Bolshevik sense of hard-line left-wingers who refuse to change.

But in the early 1980s, these atavists would miss their opportunity to play the wreckers' game in areas like the Macquarie Group's formation early in the Hawke–Keating government, partly because of the political skill of Paul Keating and partly through their own ignorance. Though they significantly outnumbered Keating and his likeminded colleagues, they were unable to thwart his capitalist reforms because their obsessions left them without an adequate comprehension of how the world had changed since the fall of Madrid, of what a floating dollar meant, of what external financial deregulation meant, and of what deregulated banking meant. Keating handled the conservative left—both parliamentarians and unionists—with superb skill. It was skill that, in part, he had accumulated during his formative battles with the left decades earlier.

LET US TRACE THESE by going back to the legendary Dr Evatt. Here was a man of baffling complexity. I do not believe that he engineered a leftwards swing in the power structure of the party as a matter of deliberate ideology or malice. He did so like a daydreamer opening a country gate and leaving it open in front of a herd of fractious cattle. He was never an ideologue in the vein of Eddie Ward, seeking to assert the supremacy of the unions in a march towards some ridiculous vision of a south sea fortress existing under utopian socialism. Evatt, in fact, was very dubious about the benefits of the powerful role that the unions played in Australian Labor. Nor was he a ranting anti-American Juan Peron. He fought hard during the formation of the United Nations to protect regional pacts from Security Council veto, so that the United States could continue its role as the protector and benefactor of Australia.

The Doc was, in many ways, a great man. A distinguished jurist, at 36 he was the youngest judge ever appointed to the High Court. After stepping down to enter federal parliament, he appeared as an advocate before his former colleagues; his most famous victory came in the challenge he mounted on behalf of the Waterside Workers Federation against the Menzies government's Communist Party Dissolution Act.

As minister for external affairs in the Chifley Labor government, he represented Australia tirelessly in the protracted negotiations to establish the United Nations. He became president of the UN General Assembly in 1948, after years spent at the negotiating table in San Francisco, fighting to prevent the institution becoming just another version of the League of Nations. Evatt was revered, particularly among the Latin American countries, for the fight he put up to secure the place of the smaller countries in the UN machinery.

He was also an author of significance. Two of his works in particular must be noted: *Rum Rebellion*, defending Governor Bligh, and *Australian Labour Leader*, defending W. A. Holman, a politician whose critics might otherwise have succeeded in confining him to the well-populated category of Labor rats. As others have observed, he was an intellectual in a party that habitually distrusted the species.

Yet he, and he alone, threw a block across the efforts of the

Catholic Church to get closer to the Labor Party, and across the efforts of young men in what were called the Industrial Groups—launched by Chifley, backed by the Catholic Church—to go into the unions and fight to clean up corruption, anti-Australian communist intrigue, and pro-Comintern ambitions. This campaign of union penetration required skill and bravery, and often incurred life-threatening danger. It was killed by a few carefully directed sentences from Dr Evatt.

I was able to view the man at firsthand in the 1955 federal election campaign, in which the Labor Party was divided along right-wing Catholic/left-wing socialist lines. This was a time before television electioneering, near the end of the long era in which press gallery journalists gathered to traverse the country, weeks before a federal election. The journalists were divided into two camps: one that followed the incumbent government leader, and the other that followed the challenging opposition leader, all over the country—to cities, big towns, and smaller towns.

I had only recently come to Canberra as a representative of Sir Frank Packer's *Daily Telegraph*. In the days before television, Packer's *Telegraph* was a powerful medium indeed. This was because, although it was fearfully biased towards Menzies, it was the workers' paper. It was an illustration of what was to happen eventually in the Soviet Union: people would rather have blue jeans than the correct party line. Working people preferred the *Telegraph*'s comics and beach girls, and the way the paper neatly folded into lunch cases, to the ponderously balanced broadsheets of the Fairfaxes and the Symes.

The *Telegraph* being what it was, I soon discovered that no self-respecting journalist wanted to go into the Labor Party domain as the newspaper's representative. For one thing, you knew you would be treated with the utmost suspicion, and for another you weren't going to get much into the paper. So there was little competition when I applied to take on the role of the Packer man with the Evatt election party. By the end of the campaign I was fonder of the opposition leader, and more bewildered by him, than I knew I should be as a young journalist under the favourable notice of Sir Frank.

Dr Evatt and his staff knew my situation: I was there to report Labor trouble, not to report Labor success. Nevertheless, I never personally experienced anything but kindness from the Doc, despite his reputation for egocentricity and for a terrible temper that he unleashed on everyone from his predecessor, Ben Chifley, to his personal staff.

He was famous for his eccentricity. Once we visited Melbourne, where the Doc spoke at a rally and tried to ameliorate the Split by calling for a party free from factional domination. But the reports in the Melbourne press the next day gave sparse attention to the Doc's argument, and much more space and weight to the interjectors.

It was the Doc's wont to pile the metropolitan papers on a stool beside him before he plunged into his morning bath. If he became enraged with the way the press had treated him, he would wildly fling divisions of the paper to the floor. This particular morning he was very angry; more or less all of the Melbourne and Sydney broadsheets were flung on the floor beside him. Dr Evatt had been a rugby league forward, characteristically playing for the Sydney University league team in a bastion of rugby union. The forward's body had become bulky over time and, when lifted from the bath at Scott's Hotel, it displaced a good deal of water that ended up on the floor.

He stood for a while and wondered if the papers still on the stool—the tabloids mainly—might have treated him better. So he turned on the water and got back into the bath, hoping to be pleasantly pleased with the difference. He wasn't. So the tabloids, piece by piece, were flung onto the floor, and his solid body displaced even more water from the bath. The reason I know about this is that as I passed the porter's desk at Scott's later that morning, a porter hailed me: 'You're with Dr Evatt's party, aren't you?'

'I'm travelling with him. Why?'

'Well, look, the housemaid on his floor is quite upset this morning. He's left an unholy mess of wet paper on the bathroom floor.'

A LITTLE OVER A YEAR BEFORE, in a single-page press statement, Evatt, apropos of nothing in particular, had announced that a group within the Victorian Labor Party was disloyal to him and to Labor, and had cost federal Labor the last election. This group was directed by *News Weekly*, virtually the official organ of Catholic Action in Victoria. Dr Evatt directed the federal Labor executive to investigate the Victorian branch to assess its domination by an outside force. This, the left-dominated federal executive enthusiastically did, and it found the Victorian branch dominated by Catholic Action.

The federal executive disqualified the Victorian branch from the 1955 federal Labor conference in Hobart, and appointed its own version of an official Victorian delegation to attend in Hobart. Hundreds of loyal Labor Party members, including existing Victorian Labor people from the federal and Victorian parliaments, were expelled. The significant casualties of the expulsions included the Cain Labor government that had run Victoria since 1952.

Why did Evatt unleash this scourge on his own party? He was of Anglo-Irish stock, descended from families more Anglican than the Archbishop of Canterbury, and exceeded only in their anti-Catholicism by the Presbyterians of Northern Ireland. So it may have been that he could not bear to see his beloved Labor Party taken over by Catholic Action. But this does not ring true to me. He was too much of an intellectual to go in for brutal sectarianism. I believe that, as the years progressed, Evatt's attractive eccentricity proceeded to the point of insanity. He became captive to the crypto-Coms and the popular fronters who had reached a point of fury at the way they were being pushed around in the unions by the Catholic-sponsored Groupers, and who decided to talk the vulnerable, flawed, egocentric, and naïve old man into precipitating a showdown with the church and the Groupers.

For generations, the Catholic Church in Australia had been loosely connected with the Labor Party because it was the party of that substantial proportion of the Australian population made up of Irish-Catholics. From the late 1940s, the church decided to make its association much closer and much more active—with good reason. The immediate post-war prime minister of Australia, Ben Chifley, had invited the church in: he perceived the escalating infiltration of the Communist Party into the Australian union movement. The church rallied to Chifley's call; not, I believe, in any predatory way. It did so because it did not want to see the party of its people overrun by the communists. The church provided money, organisation, and men to counter the communists in the unions, and it provided material support for its young men to seek pre-selection by the Labor Party for election contests.

To understand what was happening here, one must return to the war years and know that Stalingrad and other instances of Russia's resistance to Hitler had evinced considerable empathy for the Soviet Union from the Australian working class. By the late 1940s, the Communist Party was much stronger here than most realised. More importantly, it was shrewd: it saw that the singular nature of the Australian Labor movement's structure made it far more important for communists to establish power in Australian unions than it did for them to seek direct election to state and federal parliaments.

This was the labyrinthine rationale: the Australian Council of Trade Unions (ACTU) was organically dominant within the Labor Party. The ACTU had the right to nominate 80 per cent of the delegates to each state Labor Party conference. In turn, the state delegations from the conferences made up the federal conference which, through its federal executive, controlled the parliamentary parties. So if a group of unions could control the ACTU at state level, they could dictate the identity and voting intentions of 80 per cent of the state party conference, and thus the six delegates each state party sent to the federal conference. They could then control absolutely the federal party machine and, through that, the political nature of the people who stood to represent Labor in parliament. So the communists worked to control as many as they could of the unions, and they had success. By the late 1940s they controlled such key unions as the Ironworkers, the Railways, and the Clerks, among others.

The effect of the Split was profound. Catholic parliamentarians who were expelled or who resigned from the Labor Party set up a rival party known first as the Anti-Communist Labor Party and then as the Democratic Labor Party. These new parties attracted Catholics who considered themselves too sophisticated to return to vote for a party purged as the Labor Party had been; Catholics who preferred now to support the church, timid though it had been, rather than the left-tainted party.

This had three effects on the cause of those who had hoped to see the Labor Party turn towards a more family-oriented, pro-small business Christian Democrat-style party. First, it reinforced the strength of the recidivists in the party who had no wish to be transformed into anti-communists; second, it activated an historic shift away from the party of those Irish-Catholics who had progressed in the world and were waiting for an opportunity to cross over to a party more reflective of the middle class; and, third, it reinforced the strength of the Liberal–Country coalition. This latter point is anchored in the peculiar paternalism of the Australian voting system, and requires some explanation.

Traditional Irish-Catholic Australians, who had seen what had happened to their party in the Evatt explosion, may well have preferred to stay at home rather than vote at the 1955 election. But voting was not only compulsory in this country; it was also preferential.

They could vote for an Anti-Communist Labor candidate, without much hope that the candidate would be elected. They were then faced with the terrible choice of casting their second preference, knowing that this would probably be the vote that mattered. They couldn't give their second preferences to the bloody crypto-communist Evatt Labor Party. So they had no option but to desert the tradition of their fathers and give their vote to the almost equally detested Anglo-Saxon Australians of the Liberal–Country Party coalition.

In succeeding elections in the decades after the Labor Split, that is what millions of disillusioned Irish-Catholics did. The result was that, after distribution of preferences, the coalition parties received millions of votes they would not otherwise have got, thus ensuring a continuous coalition government—mostly under the leadership of Sir Robert Menzies —for almost 20 years. The remnant bunch of dreamers, trade union hacks, and truculent lefties that now constituted official Labor were left to stew and plot in negative juices, wondering about nationalisation of this industry and that, wondering about making the public service the leader of wage push in the country, and wondering about closing private schools and breaking the ties with America.

PAUL KEATING was a child of the sectarian split. He was the product of a quintessential Grouper home. Keating's father, Matt, was an Irish-descended devout Catholic member of the Labor Party and an active member of the Industrial Groups until the suddenly ascendant left of the party succeeded in having the groups banned in the middle 1950s. If the Keating family had lived in Melbourne instead of Sydney, the world would never have heard of Paul Keating. Matt would have been torn from the Labor Party by his Catholic Actionists peers falling all around him in Melbourne and pulling him down with them. Matt would have turned his support to the Anti-Communist Labor Party until, disillusioned by the pusillanimity of the church, he and the rest of its hopefuls would have drifted away from politics and concentrated on business.

Keating is presented by almost all who have anything to say about his beginnings as of 'working-class' origin. This is a misleading representation, especially for the role this book traces for him. Rather than working class, the Matt Keating family was petit bourgeois, in instincts and eventually in status. Grandfather Keating was a man of some means; and father Matt, although he slogged it out as an apprentice boilermaker and then a full tradesman for years at the Everleigh Railway Workshops in Redfern, took the opportunity, when it presented itself, to sell his car and take out a mortgage on his house in order to buy into an engineering business. This is what the bourgeois will do to buy into a business that proves a good investment, as this one did.

Again there is a requirement when talking of Keating's early days to speak of the engineering business as small. It was small to begin with. But it made essential engineering equipment for the ready-mixed concrete industry at a time when ready-mixed concrete was as common as wooden house-frames in suburban Sydney. And Matt's engineering business soon spawned a ready-mixed concrete business of its own. In sum, the Keating family business was not small; by family standards, it was substantial. It was eventually sold off, not because it wasn't successful, but first because Matt was failing in health and Paul was showing no more than modest enthusiasm for taking over the business; and, second, because its opportunities for growth required more capital.

This is not your typical background for a Labor member of parliament. But there is something to add here to explain Paul Keating's extraordinary adaptability when it came to making peak government decisions of the kind that got Macquarie Group into full stride. Unlike most Labor members of parliament, Paul had been schooled by his father, Matt, with a respect for markets and the merits of honest business activity; in fact, Paul had considered a career in the ready-mixed concrete business. But already laid out for him was a career in federal politics. And few, given the choice, are likely to set aside the excitement of a career in federal politics for even the most rewarding and honourable career in ready-mixed concrete; certainly not someone as imaginative and bold as Keating. By the age of 20, Keating was already a battle-hardened factional warrior with a skill for strategy.

Examined adequately, all these things add up to explain why Paul Keating in the middle 1980s opted for action that would open up markets for the likes of Macquarie Group, without a source of inducement other than the intellectual satisfaction to be gained and a predilection for Napoleonic decision-making.

In the months following the purge within Labor, the political Catholics of Victoria found heart in the assumption that their brothers in New South Wales would take an early opportunity to rise, declare themselves anti-communist Labor and, at the next election, sweep Evatt Labor away to the status of a rump and then proceed to restore official Labor to a Christian, anti-communist creed. But the New South Wales right failed to rise in support of their Victorian co-religionists. It was better, they thought, to fight on within the Labor Party as it was. So while the right became a rump party in the Victorian, Tasmanian, and federal parliaments, the faction continued to flourish in New South Wales. Following in the footsteps of his father, Matt, Paul Keating emerged within the party as a young prince within the Labor right.

It is usual for successful politicians to learn gradually how to present as leaders in public, how to convey to others both a sense of humour and senses of distaste, how to inject excitement and enthusiasm, how to employ sardonic wit as a signal of knowingness and strength; as it happens, it was the absence of learning and guile in these modes that made Sir Garfield Barwick and Tom Hughes, both outstanding jurists, complete flops as politicians.

Over time, successful politicians learn when to come down very heavy and when to lightly finesse, when to talk strongly and when to keep quiet. Then, perhaps after ten to 15 years of gradually testing oneself in these and other things, one knows whether one has what it takes. The defining thing about Paul Keating is that he was given the opportunity by special circumstances to test himself on all these matters and more before he was twenty-one.

The young political Catholics of New South Wales faced a savage blooding on all aspects of politics in a singular time in the 1960s. From the outside, they found themselves reviled as traitors by their kin in Victoria and Tasmania. The New South Wales Catholics knew that, although they had elected not to publicly split the party in 1955, to save their souls they had to internalise the fight, and that is how the young Paul Keating became swept up in the most savage internal party factional war that has ever occurred in Australian politics.

The fight within the New South Wales party was between the left, which had prevailed in the Evatt split and the Catholic right wing which ostensibly had been defeated. Within New South Wales Labor, it was the determination of the Catholic right never to be defeated. The fight began in the state party's youth group which met once a fortnight at the party's offices in Elizabeth Street, Sydney, to the accompaniment of the bashing of boots upon the floor, the banging of chairs, and vitriolic abuse between the two divisions, the Catholics and the Coms. When you came to the youth group, you came to Donnybrook Fair.

To bring the youth council under control, senior Labor

Party politicians decided it had to have new leadership—young people who were showing some promise of performing like politicians rather than rabble-rousers. From this decision Paul Keating emerged as president of the youth council, and he and his coterie successfully ran the council through the latter 1960s. In this setting, Keating not only honed his political skills, but also cultivated the connections he was going to need to propel him to becoming the youngest member of federal parliament in 1969.

For this rapid elevation, to have been stamped a political leader in the youth council was not enough: one had to have the numbers for pre-selection out in the branches. Here the same internal right-wing/left-wing rivalry prevailed. No matter how promising the contender, in a party so divided there was no question of him or her being handed pre-selection on a platter. It had to be won. Paul Keating chose in 1967 to build his Catholic-dominated branch of Bankstown into the core he would need to be pre-selected for the federal seat of Banks. He had the good fortune to have as his father not a working-class boiler-maker, but a successful bourgeois businessman with a businessman's capacity to organise and run the machinery necessary to get a 23-year-old ensconced as the candidate for an area in which a left-wing candidate remained the incumbent.

The command post for Matt Keating's drive to establish Paul was St Brendan's Catholic Church in Bankstown. From here he organised enough new members to drive out the startled left-wing incumbent. All seemed to be going well until, like an act of God, the Australian Electoral Commission undertook one of its periodic reviews of electoral boundaries across the nation, and decided that the Keating headquarters of Bankstown Central was to be shifted into the neighbouring electorate of

Blaxland. This was not at the behest of any political party. It was beyond parties; it was a constitutional matter. Fortunately, Australia was and is sufficiently clean as a democracy that gerrymandering is impossible. The Electoral Commission is left to operate entirely above the fray, and major shifts in electoral boundaries can and do take place as population changes in a changing nation.

But, for the Keatings, the change in boundaries was a blow. With precious little time left before the next federal election, Paul and his camp had to quickly decide whether to move with St Brendan's and the Bankstown Central branch into the remote territory of the electorate of Blaxland, or to stay and re-organise in the seat of Banks. The problems were several: although there was a substantial advantage in joining St Brendan's in the shift to Blaxland, there were also substantial disadvantages. The seat of Blaxland already had a sitting Labor member in the form of the slumbering, yet fondly regarded, Eli Harrison. Blaxland was also home territory for an army of left-wingers. It was the time of the Vietnam War, and the divisions within New South Wales Labor were rising to a crescendo. But, on balance, the Keating camp concluded that it must move with St Brendan's across to the seat of Blaxland.

It was no longer right wing against left wing out there in the Sydney Labor electorates; it was, in the parlance of the participants, Catholic against Com. In their fury against each other, each side would stop at nothing. In their first moves against one another in Blaxland, the left moved to have the incumbents of St Brendan's and Bankstown Central declared ineligible to vote in the pre-selection process because party rules required the branch to have been operating in the electorate for twelve months before the pre-selection vote. On technical grounds, St Brendan's and Bankstown Central would therefore be ineligible.

It became necessary for the Keating forces to move the whole of their carefully nurtured membership from the relocated Bankstown Central branch into the less welcoming and bolshie branch of Condell Park. The left challenged the legitimacy of Bankstown Central members transferring to Condell Park. And it did subsequently appear that many of the transfers breached another rule of the party, namely that a member of a branch could not vote in a pre-selection unless he had been a member of that branch for at least a year before preselection.

The Keating forces ruthlessly settled the first of their difficulties in the seat of Blaxland by having Harrison's endorsement dumped. But the matter of the transfer of members from Bankstown Central to Condell Park was something else. On the night of the pre-selection vote, the returning officer, one Murt O'Brien, appointed by the party to oversee the voting in Blaxland, decided to separate the votes of new members of Condell Park into a closely guarded separate pile. With these hived off, the pre-selection vote came out 124 for the left-winger, Bill Junor, a teaching fellow in economics at the University of New South Wales, and 108 for Paul Keating, with a package of 49 votes challenged and uncounted. It was Murt O'Brien's intention to take these home with him that night and to consult the party the next day on what should be done about them.

But the Keating family immediately demonstrated its political insights: Paul quickly made it clear that Murt O'Brien was not going to leave the Blaxland Scout Hall, where the votes for Condell Park were being counted, without opening that package and counting the 49 votes within it. When Murt resisted and declared Bill Junor the provisional winner, the Keating camp—in the early hours of the morning— contacted the party's state returning officer and demanded his attention to the matter. The state returning officer declined to attend, saying it could wait till later that day. The Keating camp, however, had a fair idea what might happen to Murt O'Brien and his vital package as he wended his way home, or even after he got home.

The leadership of the left at the hall were probably even then filling in 49 forms, leaving only names to be added. If Murt were to be let out of the hall with his package, who knew what untoward setback might occur? He might have had an accident on the way home, in which the package was temporarily lost and the names on the voting sheets were quickly transposed to new sheets. He might have become lost in the dimly-lit early-morning streets. Or, once he got home and got to sleep, he might have suffered a cat-like intruder and burglary in which the package of 49 was temporarily taken. The package might not even have had to leave the house for the damage to be done.

The reluctance of the New South Wales returning officer to attend was met by movement further up the hierarchical tree. The Keating camp brought in federal Labor Party leadership. This resulted in the rapid attendance of New South Wales officials with jumpers and pants pulled rapidly over their pyjamas. With shared responsibility, the New South Wales returning officer and his lieutenants took over the package of 49 votes. A week later, the official result came from the party headquarters: Keating 145; Junor 125. Keating was on his way as the official Labor candidate in the safe seat of Blaxland.

Other successful politicians might wait 15 years before they got anything like the seasoning that Paul Keating experienced when he was hardly out of adolescence. He was a tough, guileful, cunning, formidable political leader. But, intellectually, he was an unknown quantity. He had finished his formal education at the age of fourteen. He had left De La Salle College Bankstown after completing his Intermediate Certificate; this was a common procedure then for those who were considered likely to follow a trade. Afterwards he did a few subjects outside school in a dilettantish sort of way. But as a youth and a young man, he never seriously faced the challenge of tough tertiary education; he was too busy elsewhere.

So he sailed through early adulthood wondering occasionally how he would have fared as a student of economics or law at university. He was still wondering when he became a minister of the Crown in federal parliament at the age of 31.

Chapter 4

The Party Persuader

'One change always leaves the way open for the establishment of others.' –Niccolo Machiavelli

PAUL KEATING'S RUSH TO GET TO THE TOP ECHELONS OF the Labor Party at an early age was, as it turned out, of debatable value. Although it gave him a tactical edge that few could approach, it robbed him of the time needed for acquiring formal academic discipline. The journey he made to develop an adequately trained mind took far longer than would have been the case had he gone to Sydney or New South Wales University as a mature student; say at the age of 19 or twenty.

It is possible that, had he done this, he might not have gone into politics. I am not suggesting that he would have turned to a traditional middle-class career in law, medicine, or business management, or to an academic career; the latter, in particular, he would have found stifling. For those who are brave, unconventional, intellectually gifted, and educated to the point of supreme self-confidence, there is a broader path available than the single furrow of a career in politics, the professions, or the academy.

The British polymath Jonathan Miller is an example of those who follow an ever-widening way. He spent a considerable time at university qualifying at one thing and another; most particularly, he qualified in natural sciences and as a doctor of medicine, and for a couple of years he practised as a doctor. But at the same time he played a role in the great revolution in British comedy of the 1960s and 1970s, through his involvement in the Cambridge Footlights and the Edinburgh Fringe. He was invited to become editor and presenter for BBC TV's arts program *Monitor*. He became a significant writer over a variety of fields; a theatre director of the first rank; and, with limited knowledge of the art form, an outstanding director of opera. He made enough money to cover his wants, but he never made the making of money, or academic advancement, political preferment, or business achievement an end in itself. Today, Miller appears to combine all his courses in a glorious mixture—medicine, mathematics, literature, music, and theatre. He is a contemporary renaissance man.

One senses that Keating would have liked to have been a renaissance man, too, and perhaps he could have been an Australian version of one if he had started earlier on the intellectual education of young Paul. He was hungry for all sorts of knowledge, game enough to act on it, and possessed instinctive insight into how one change could open up much broader avenues of action. For the next 20 years, he followed his own process of intellectual development. He chose his mentors and he changed them; and, as he leaned more towards men who were intellectually sophisticated, his own thought became more rigorous, complex, and sweeping. By early middle age he could produce explanations for the way the world worked that were remarkable for their breadth and internal consistency. He became fascinated with the forces that were governing Australia in the second half of the twentieth century, developing a readiness to interfere with them, to pull the levers, with a determination to do so powerfully enough to change the outlook for a nation.

By the 1990s he was still, by temperament, a thorough-going Labor man, largely because he detested the pomposity he found on the conservative side of politics. But, intellectually, he had become agnostic: Labor ideology had ceased to infect his opinions and analysis. He formulated policy in a realm above the party-political, where the processes of social and economic engineering could be honed until he personally considered them workable and worthy. Almost all his views in this realm were market-oriented.

Keating must have been able to stand off from himself before he was 40 and to know objectively that he had an intelligence and craft only given to great generals. At the very least, he must have begun to feel he had Napoleonic powers. As chance would have it, his groping towards a political economics of rationality and his own sense of strength coincided with the outbreak of energy and impatience that was occurring among Australian youth in an area outside politics—the world of finance. There, a force of young people in a field of play quite different from Keating's was breaking at last in disillusionment from the old conservatives. Together, the two forces—creative politics and creative finance—combined to create a phenomenon which most of us have not yet grasped.

THE MOST DANGEROUS PERIOD for Keating's intellectual development was when he first came to Canberra as the youngest member of the House of Representatives and, for the want of better company, fell under the influence of Labor people who were a generation older. He was particularly taken with the style and economic philosophy of Rex Connor, minister for minerals and energy in the Whitlam government.

Connor, a crazy old patriot, will be remembered in history as the man who sent a mysterious Pakistani named Tirath Khemlani into the souks and bazaars of Arabia in quest of the largest loan he could lay his hands on for the Commonwealth of Australia. The minister had a detailed knowledge of Australia's mineral and energy resources, and a bold plan. It was his belief that we should face the rest of the world with our resources piled behind us, and stand as a bull-terrier guard dog does when it faces the street. We should have no truck with international private enterprise. We should develop our resources with our own public-sector loan money, under public-sector ownership, with no share of ownership going to non-Australians. Paul Keating's enthusiastic association with Rex Connor stands as an embarrassment to his later friends and mentors in Treasury, the Reserve Bank, and elsewhere, blessed as they were with finely trained minds.

The association must be taken as the low point of Keating's intellectual development. When Labor went into opposition after Whitlam, Keating became shadow minister for minerals and energy, and there gained an entirely different perspective. He met and learned from the likes of Sir James Foots of Mount Isa Mines, Sir Ian McLennan of BHP, Sir Frank Espie of Bougainville Copper, and Sir Roderick Carnegie of CRA (later Rio Tinto). Exposure to these men led him into a real world of global risk-capital, global markets, and global cycles, and to the limitations of public ownership policy in Australia. He began to lift himself above the mire of semi-ignorance and prejudice in which Labor ideologues of the time often lived.

The next step along Keating's singular path of education came from a personal encounter with the Australian banks. This originated in the interest he had continued to take in the family firm, Marlak. When the government of Malaysia asked the company to apply its expertise in the development of Malaysia's tin-dredging industry, Keating senior and junior took a Malaysian letter along to their bank, which happened to be the English Scottish and Australian Bank, a substantial part of the Australian banking oligopoly that has since merged with the ANZ Bank. This letter was from the Malaysian government, indicating its desire to employ Marlak in some innovative work in tin dredging.

It was a letter of intent, in business terms—an asset, in that it showed a sovereign government's desire to do business with the Keating family firm. The Keatings needed all the credit they could get if they were going to bring off the venture. The ES&A Bank told them it would lend 60 per cent against the value of all the land, buildings, and equipment of Marlak and the assets of its shareholders. The bank offered nothing on the value of the letter; its lending managers didn't want to hear about cash-flow lending. This was an outrageously stingy banking approach to helping—or not helping—an established client that had been presented with a relatively risk-free opportunity to expand and transform its business. But it was a typical bank response of the late 1970s.

Marlak didn't win the loan or the project, and the experience left Keating with a determination to reform the Australian banking system, to make it more open and accountable. He could see that its traditional modus operandi was constraining the growth of the Australian economy.

'When I became shadow minister for national resources in the latter 1970s I used my position to pursue this intolerable weakness vigorously,' he told me some time later. 'In a speech in the House, I told the country that the monopoly position given to Australia's six banks [soon to merge into four, thus leading to the concept of Australia's 'four pillars' banking system] had created the most conservative banking system in the world. In my position as shadow minister for national resources, I told the House that the existing bank structure was retarding this young country's massive minerals endowment, and as soon as I got the chance I was going to do something about it.

'I mused at the time that the answer to this problem was the opening up of bank licensing to international competition—so that the smug executives who had rejected the excellent Marlak proposition would have to get out and compete, instead of having their business given to them on a plate by the provisions of the Banking Act.

'Well, this quickly provoked a reaction from one Douglas Stride, the managing director of the Commercial Bank of Australia. In a letter to all branches, he pronounced that my speech meant that foreign banks would be permitted into Australia should Labor gain office. This, he said, would be a terrible thing because it would place the banks' most important profit areas at risk. Marginal profit areas with correspondingly high staff numbers would have to be reassessed, Stride said, as the banks would have to restructure their operations to meet competition and loss of income. In other words, he was responding to me with a blatant threat: allow more bank competition, and they would sack a lot of people.

'It was pretty small-minded stuff. And, sure enough, the

hammering upon me from the bank unions commenced soon thereafter.'

Keating proceeded from this experience with his family bank and his face-off with the banks en bloc to formulate his first major economic treatise. Others were to come, and they had to be honed on the expertise of the particular group of friends I mention below. This was how his intellectual development proceeded in these years: a challenge or an inspiration would come out of left field or right field—for example, Rex Connor's Fortress Australia view of developing the nation's mineral and energy wealth would seize him. Then the mining establishment would rebut that challenge. Out of these would come a dialectic that established a net intellectual gain.

Initially, there was too much hubris in his responses: for example, his quick embrace of the truculent theories of Rex Connor contained a fair amount of Irish trailing of the coat. He would seize hold of an idea, because ideas were like armour or weapons. But, under guidance, he learned more and more how to satisfy himself about the internal consistency of an inclination before taking it further and moulding it into a belief. Eventually he changed his mode sufficiently so that he could think about a surprise development, a shock, or a poke in the eye, in order to deal with it rationally.

The next big step in his development was that he would formulate a thesis arising from these things. Then he would have the thesis checked by the half-dozen top economists from Treasury and the Reserve Bank who were his special friends now, only too happy to make themselves available: in Treasury, Dr Chris Higgins, Ted Evans, Bernie Fraser, Tony Cole, and David Morgan; and, at the Reserve Bank, Bob Johnston and Aussie Holmes.

The Keating thesis arising from the commercial banks' argument ran like this: for some 100 years between about 1880 and 1980 Australia had run on what he at first called the economic-defence model. It had three legs to it, so he then called it the tripod model. One leg was the big and strong terms of trade, made up of gold, minerals, wool, and wheat—as a result of which prices for the things we exported kept moving up more than the prices of the things we imported, thus substantially and almost continuously increasing our real income. It was here that the traditional banks made their fortune, financing the transfer of the big wool clip from sheep stations to the mills and processors of Bradford, and financing the shipping of gold to the Bank of England; of ferrous and non-ferrous metals across the world; and of Australian hard wheat to the seekers of high-protein bread across the world.

This solid leg of the three-legged stool paid for the second leg, which allowed us to develop manufacturing industries domestically behind high tariffs. And that, in turn—in a relationship known to historians as New Protection—allowed a third leg, which was high wages for Australian unionists. Australia's banks were the acolytes of the model, and it required no more than a few dull, unadventurous banks to avoid rocking the boat and to do what was needed here. On this tripod the nation sat securely for a century.

The key to it was the comity and preservation of established forces so that each of the parties could take its cut out of the system without too much fuss. The farmers and graziers and miners had their cut as the nobles of the system; the manufacturers had their cut, courtesy of tariff protection; and the unions had their bit, courtesy of protection and arbitrated wages. A certain amount of ambition for the lower ranks was taken care of by the system: those in the union movement who decided they wanted to be upwardly mobile had the continuous prospect of finishing up as vice-presidents of the Arbitration Commission and the like, where they would meet and mix with representatives of the employer groups. Such ambition everywhere was carefully watched, and not too much of it was encouraged.

It was a dull, tight little island run as a conspiracy against the population as a whole. The people who caught no more than the crumbs off the table were the ordinary men and women getting nowhere, and paying twice as much as they should for cars, for shares, and for just about everything. The conspiracy of mediocrity was important here, so that the spirit of wage indexation could prevail and you could have a very good tradesman working his life out on the same rate of pay as the nong next to him. There was no tolerance for within-sector wage flexibility, and this extended itself to an absence of premium on innovation, work effort, or brilliance generally. This went on for generations.

Tracing his model out over time, Keating would come to the part where—around the time Bob Menzies decided to retire and take up his post as Lord Warden of the Cinque Ports—the tripod began to fall apart because the long period of benign terms of trade began to change. Everything we sold abroad started to become cheap, while the things we bought from abroad grew more expensive—colour televisions, videotape recorders, electronic goods generally. In economic terms, the external deficit or current account deficit, which had remained at around 2.5 per cent of national income as long as the tripod held stable, began to grow significantly. This was something that couldn't go on.

Keating said, 'I began to realise that the tripod model was essentially a spoof on those of us who weren't in on the game. The trouble was that all three points of party political power were getting their bit out of it—the Liberal Party, the Labor Party, the Country Party, and if you spoke up against it you were the odd man out.

'This came home to me in a debate within the Labor Party's federal conference in Canberra in 1985. The debate was about opening up the Australian banking system to more licensed domestic banks and to foreign banks. To me, this step was crucial to get away from the tripod model and start a new economic life for Australia. But there was strong feeling in the Labor Party against freeing up the banking system like this, and I had to get the idea through the federal conference. The assault on my move to endorse the entry of foreign banks was led by Jack Ferguson, leader of the left in New South Wales, and deputy premier there.

'Jack said to the meeting, "Well, if it comes to the choice between foreign banks and Australian banks, I'm with the Australian banks every time." In other words, here's the old leftie getting up and siding with Sir Robert Law Smith of the National Australia Bank, Sir Noel Foley of Westpac Bank, Charles Berenson Goode of the ANZ Bank, and so on. So there it was: you had the trade unions on the left making common cause with the old-established order of finance, because they were both fundamental elements and beneficiaries of the tripod system. If you wanted to up-end that system you were in for it. Just to underscore the point, I remember the bank union coming back on me again in Canberra and telling me that I shouldn't be making the kind of speeches I was making.'

In the face of such Labor conservatism, how did Keating and

Hawke manage to carry out their agenda for radical financial reform? A necessary but not sufficient condition was the fear within the new federal Labor government that early mistakes would set them tumbling towards the same self-destructive fate that had befallen Whitlam Labor a decade before. It was this trepidation that caused the honourable members to sit open-mouthed and listen in amazement as Keating reeled off the kind of free-market things he was going to do early in the life of the government. He and Hawke were going to expose the banks to international competition. They were going to deregulate the banking system. They were going to free-float the Australian dollar without any fallback. They were going to remove all restrictions on capital flows to and from Australia. They were going to finish the freeing of trade in government bonds. They were going to open home-funding to all comers. They were going to steadily lower tariffs on Australian production.

To bring all this off without causing a destructive reaction would seem to require a Benjamin Franklin or a Lloyd George. Years later, I asked Ted Evans, secretary of the Treasury and then chairman of Westpac Bank, about the importance of Keating in this Australian setting.

'He was unique as a persuader within his party,' Evans said. 'He didn't try to work as an orator. He worked by knowing his audience, by equipping himself with a thorough knowledge of what it would take to have that audience go along with him. For example, from the first day he came into power as treasurer, it was Treasury's priority to warn him that the budget deficit must come down. His first response was to say that he needed an argument to put to the Labor caucus about this. "They don't have any innate preference towards getting deficits down," he said. "In fact, perhaps the contrary. You give me an argument for doing this, and I will work on them." So I worked to give him the argument I thought he should have.

'He sent my paper back and said, "I don't fully understand this myself. I know my audience, and I know this won't go over with caucus. Try again." I sent a second minute, and he sent that back. On the third try, he was happy. So I wrote him a presentation for caucus. But he sat down and wrote it out in long hand into his own words. He had an ability to know what he didn't understand and to admit this, and to know what his audience required. When he went to the caucus he took me along to sit in the background. And as I listened to him present it I thought to myself, I could not have hit the mark as nicely as he did. I saw immediately what he meant by knowing his audience.'

Ask just about any ordinary citizen who remembers Paul Keating speaking off-the-cuff, and ask what they thought about him, and they are likely to say they remember a man who spoke fluently, but who spoke like the Bastard from the Bush. In parliament, he once described Malcolm Fraser as a man with his arse stuffed with razorblades. Billie Snedden, the short-lived coalition leader who preceded Fraser, was immortalised as 'a carcass swinging in the breeze that no one had gotten round to cutting down'. And outside the House, after a party meeting, Keating rebuked a couple of his own colleagues: 'I go out for a piss and you pull this one on me. Well, this is the last time I leave you alone. From now on I'll stick to you like shit to a blanket.'

But while Keating often speaks with a rough idiom that can be very cruel, he is more sophisticated than most of us. It is one of the enigmas attaching to Keating that he allowed the general public understanding of his persona to develop as it has. In Evans' words, 'Paul Keating is innately intelligent. He is very largely self-educated; beyond economics he is educated in history, in his love of French art, in architecture, in almost anything French. But more than being intelligent, he knew how to learn.

'Over the years, I watched him address varieties of people. I watched him address the Labor caucus. I saw him address business people. I saw him address arts people. He was a different person each time. He would speak at the levels and about the things he judged to be right. He showed quite an extraordinary ability: I have never seen a politician become so effective and acquire such extraordinary learning.'

In time, then, Paul Keating acquired a comprehension broad enough to allow him to think as a visionary, but that is still something poorly understood by most of his compatriots.

DURING ALL THAT KEATING DID in the 1980s, the long grind of animosity between him and the banks of the 'four pillars' regime went on. These banks showed themselves ready to hold their privileged positions by hook or by crook.

In 1985, the Hawke–Keating government had brought the banks' hubris to a crescendo with its announcement that it had licensed 16 foreign banks to operate within Australia. Some foreign banks came for a while and then backed out. Given the sound and the fury that had accompanied this entry of foreign banks, the outcome was curious. Had the claim of inadequate bank competition in Australia been a furphy? Not really. What happened was a unified show by the four pillars that they were not done yet with Keating and the government. As a counter to the Hawke–Keating policy moves, the Australian banks began expanding credit at a suicidal rate; they expanded credit so fast that new foreign bank entrants had no room to move in Australia. The only new bank that survived was Macquarie Group, which had been granted a domestic licence. The banks' response, suddenly unleashing a welter of credit to domestic and business consumers, became the underlying concern to the government throughout the 1980s.

Said Paul Keating: 'The old domestic banks went like charging bulls into credit expansion from 1985 on, as a means of keeping the foreigners out: they went flat out to prevent foreign banks getting any market share through 1985, 1986, 1987, 1988, and 1989. They did this at the expense of their book quality. They expanded credit at twice the value of nominal gross domestic product—20 per cent as against 10 per cent. And in a sense they won. Eventually, they had us in a position where we dared not check them lest they failed. Westpac and the ANZ virtually did fail: the government and the Reserve Bank had to hold them together until they got back on their feet. There was an obvious time in the 1980s to stop this credit creation, but no one would stop.'

Keating called this the adolescent phase of his reformation: in this phase, the banks almost burned the place down.

Credit poured into commercial property in Australia at a rate never seen before or since. The amount of commercial property built rose sixfold as a proportion of national product between 1980 and 1990. The price of Australian commercial property rose from an index figure of 30 in 1980 to more than 150 by 1990. At the same time, Australian companies used abundant credit to bid for greater and greater size. Attempting to take over BHP was no problem for Robert Holmes à Court. A 'tomorrow the world' concept was no problem for Rupert

Murdoch. The picture of himself as a global asset holder was no problem for Alan Bond. At their height in the 1980s, his companies owned airships, diamond mines, entertainment complexes, television empires, and international brewing complexes. He owned the St Moritz Hotel in New York and Van Gogh's *Irises*.

In the midst of all this, Keating and Hawke were trying to hold a wages accord engineered by themselves and the chief of the Australian Council of Trade Unions, Bill Kelty. In this, they succeeded remarkably well.

'The unions were holding to an ask of about 6 per cent increase a year,' said Paul Keating. 'But bank credit was continuing to expand at such a pace that this couldn't hold. It's a tribute to the union leadership of Bill Kelty that it held as well as it did. If we had yielded at that point in the wage accord we would have gone back to where Howard left us in 1982 with double-digit wages growth and double-digit inflation. As it was, in the midst of this credit surge, the underlying inflation rate was 4 per cent.'

Paul Keating had entered government nurturing his theorem of a century-old Australian tripod, the workings of which had required the subjugation of Australian households to meet the needs of an established combination: the export industries, the overly tariff-protected manufacturing industries, and the overly protected Australian unions. The essence of his mission in those first six years had been to ease this ancient burden on ordinary working-class and middle-class households.

And in this he succeeded impressively. The banks' strategy to keep out foreign newcomers involved strong competition against unlanded foreigners, which involved the reversal of the old tripod-era gap between the price the banks paid for money and the price at which they sold it. This forced a movement in the price of bank money in favour of private consumers. The narrowing of domestic bank margins represented a big transfer of income from the banks to households by the 1990s.

In this same period, tariffs were cut, on average by one-third. These things, particularly the tariff cuts, took time to work through to households, but by the middle 1990s a very large shift in income from over-protected industries, banks, and unions had occurred in Australia, the effect of which is still being felt. For the last 15 years, the propelling power behind the Australian economy has been the shift in incomes and asset values to the household sector. The bum space upon the stool above the tripod has become smaller and smaller, and its legs less and less secure.

While Paul Keating was battling the banking establishment, Macquarie Group was on its way to becoming the most valuable share on the Australian stock market. Once Labor made it clear that it was going to open up the Australian economy, David Clarke and his colleagues decided they had better urgently organise their transformation of Hill Samuel Australia into a licensed Australian bank. They needed to raise an amount of capital equivalent to 70 per cent of the market value of the infant bank to buy out the parent company.

Although Hill Samuel had shown itself as a real comer, the expanded operations and expanded capital base that it now needed was regarded cautiously by the Australian market. The buy-back was no shoo-in. The requirement was not just that the foreign voting stock had to be cut to 15 per cent from 100 per cent; the reclaimed 70 per cent also had to be in a form that could not overwhelm or instruct the new bank; this would allow what was to be the Macquarie bank culture and Macquarie bank staff to prevail in decision-making: a solid block of ownership could neither be in the hands of foreign-owned firms or powerful individual local firms. This was a big ask: it meant that the Macquarie Group people had to eschew institutions and companies looking for influence and immediate returns.

The first 35 percentage points of the required 70 came without too much grind. But it was soon apparent that the remaining 35 per cent would be tough. The bank staff as a group came to the party by cashing in their profit shares and options to make up 15 percentage points of the required 35. The last 20 percentage points were the struggle, but the bank did not compromise: it refused to accept capital seeking any degree of direct control, and it did not accept capital seeking quick returns. But, as it neared capital completion, it found itself like the husband who declares he will not give an inch in an argument with his wife and then decides he must arrive the next evening with roses in his hand.

So, in its first years of operating as a bank, Macquarie felt itself obliged to deliver outstanding prizes. The initial projects it chose had to be of such quality and earnings level as to outshine the whole market. This came first in the form of a New South Wales government project to build the toll way from Castle Hill to the city. It was a gem. And through all the disasters of Sydney tunnels and toll ways, the Hills motorway has remained a shining example. It had not been running long before it was able to list on the stock exchange as a separate entity, selling at a premium as one of the best investments its participants ever made.

Macquarie Group moved quickly to repeat the Sydney performance in Melbourne. The Transurban toll way emerged as a world-class endeavour. Again, value was established by a level of earnings above the Commonwealth bond rate, and again the venture was floated at a premium as a stand-alone package on the share market. As a blue-chip entrepreneur and financial engineer, Macquarie's name was made in Australia. To keep up the momentum, it looked around to other states, but at that point could find no further takers from outside New South Wales and Victoria.

Since its days as a subsidiary of Hill Samuel, it had had an Australian presence in London. Now it quickly augmented this with people who were familiar with the Hills motorway and the Transurban toll way, and these people came up with a British government project to build a major bypass structure around Manchester. Once again, Macquarie produced a gem. Returns were more than good enough to warrant an early stand-alone listing at a premium on the London Stock Exchange.

Macquarie was on its way internationally: it was hardly a household name but, among those whose business it was to judge these things, Macquarie was a real comer, not only in Australia but in the world. From the Manchester bypass, Macquarie—by this time under the aegis of a newly created division named Macquarie Infrastructure Group—quickly spread its toll roads and tunnelling business to South Korea, Canada, Indiana, Chicago, and San Diego.

PAUL KEATING'S SUPERANNUATION REFORMS, outlined in the next chapter, would feed the Macquarie machine with the investment funds it needed to grow and prosper. But other reforms would also help drive the rapid expansion of the Australian stock market and the Australian financial services industry in the 1980s and 1990s.

As he went along in Treasury, Keating became more and more focused on the tax system, particularly the company-tax system. He formulated his own economic framework for Australia, and tax policy was a vital part of it. He needed to control tax policy at the wage-earner level to allow him to give unions the choice of accepting a cut in tax or taking that cut in that particular year as a contribution to superannuation rather than as cash in hand.

For six months, there was a struggle within the Labor government as to whether Paul Keating or Ralph Willis—Treasury or the department of finance—would control taxation policy. Keating was determined to win. He grasped that this was much more than a matter of controlling wage and salary tax for superannuation policy purposes; it was also a matter of controlling company tax for total-strategy purposes.

For decades, investors in Australian companies had paid tax twice on company incomes. They had paid it in the form of company tax when company income was declared, and they had paid it again in the form of personal income tax when company income was distributed.

For generations of mostly right-wing treasurers, the Australian capitalist had gone on blindly paying tax twice on his equity capital. This was largely because conservative treasurers had been too lazy or incompetent to pick up the anomaly, and because it didn't suit public servants to point it out. Seeing what had been happening for so long, Keating stepped in smartly to correct it. He did this not because of any perverse pang of sympathy for the people whom he regarded as class enemies, but because the business-tax arrangement as it stood was robbing Australian equities, Australian capital markets, of their attraction, and thus robbing the Australian economy of support. He could see that if investors were taxed only once they would have more capital to invest, and would invest it more willingly.

During a conversation I had with Keating over Chinese tea in the old Tang Dynasty restaurant in Canberra, during his period between being treasurer and becoming prime minister, he said to me: 'I've done more for companies here than any conservative government has done. And I hope I will be remembered here as the treasurer—after all these conservative treasurers and prime ministers—who finally got share capital to being taxed only once. And, through that, for share income in superannuation funds to being taxed only once.

'Let me explain it to you. Under the system that prevailed before me, let's start with $100 in company income under the treasurership of Howard, say—initial company tax was 46 per cent. So that left $54 dollars of after-tax income. You distributed that to the shareholders, and the distributed income was taxed again at 60 per cent. So what the owners of the company got was $22 out of the original gross income.

'If you didn't distribute the income, your company was hit by the undistributed profits tax, which was also 60 per cent. This was an impossible setting for any company wanting to grow, and it was crazy for an economy needing to grow rapidly like ours.

'So I reduced the initial company tax rate to 36 per cent, leaving $64 net company income available. And then I abolished the undistributed profits tax. This meant I had near enough to treble the amount the company could retain as after-tax income. And if they then paid out this undistributed income to their shareholders, the shareholders got an imputed credit for the 36 per cent tax their company had already paid.

'The corporate sector was at last in a position to grow rapidly. Successful private companies like, for example, Visy Board, were at last in a position to grow into major companies on the share market.'

Keating had pulled out his pen and begun scribbling his figures on a paper napkin. The napkin was too soft, so he had seized the menu. 'Let me show you this, David,' he said. I stopped him writing and called for the urgent supply of some blank paper. He was illustrating to me the importance of advancing the company-tax reform and the pension-funds revolution together. He was to make the returns from a successful company superior to other investments. More and more, it would be the superannuation funds that were the investors benefiting from this. Wage-earner contributions aside, these funds would be getting richer and richer from dividends and imputed tax payments.

Unlike such things as the floating of the dollar, this matter of company-tax change was not something that Keating could precipitate into policy by the rush of events. The company-tax part of his blueprint for change was something that had to be meticulously cleared through the caucus. Tax was something that Ralph Willis had intended to be part of his Finance ministry, as compensation for Paul Keating taking the Treasury, so this was an area of well-telegraphed party sensitivity.

It had to be taken through caucus with care to ensure a unanimous endorsement of what Keating was doing. Given the nature of caucus, the mere sound of something like company-tax relief rang alarm bells. As Keating himself remarked on another occasion: 'Labor caucus members don't exactly identify with people who receive dividends.'

I remembered Ted Evans' illustration to me of Keating's

ability to communicate, when he chose to, on quite different levels and in different spheres. One of Ted's pictures was Keating working on the caucus.

Paul's sale of the company-tax changes to a sceptical, almost baleful, caucus was a nice example of this. He asked caucus members to place themselves in the position of a small shopkeeper—not the clambering Anglo trying to move up the line, but perhaps an Italian or a Pakistani content to be of service to a working-class community.

If such a mum and dad had incorporated themselves against liability under existing law, they got taxed twice—once at the company tax rate and then, once the income was distributed to them, at the full personal rate. Did caucus think that was equitable to people who were likely to support the Labor Party? No, they concluded, they didn't. So you must accept, Keating told them, that the new equity must be extended through the system as a whole.

Back at the Tang Dynasty, Keating continued: 'You see, Kelty undertook that over five years—that is, by now—he would have achieved by industrial award negotiations a union-based superannuation system equivalent to 3 per cent of income. And I said then that if you can do that—and that is what he has done—you can tell your members that the Commonwealth will legislate an incentive scheme for the employers to put in on behalf of the workers. So that we have a 6 per cent of income for workers' superannuation made up of workers' contributions and employers'. This will be joined by a Commonwealth co-payment in the form of tax cuts to the workers given on the condition that the cut is taken in the form of superannuation rather than cash in hand. This would rise by 1 per cent a year until it reaches a cut-off point of 15 per cent of superannuation by 1999/2000.'

Two things considered here appear unrelated: one, the reform of company taxation to the point where dividends could flow in maximum amounts to the shareholder; the other, the reform of industrial-pension legislation whereby tax cuts could flow directly to the benefit of a fund member. Put together, these two things can be seen as a dynamic combination. Whether Keating saw them from the start as such, I don't know. But he grasped their interrelation soon enough, and this capacity to see a dynamic whole and its consequences well before others is part of what marks him as a singular man.

Chapter 5

The Golden Circle

'Out of intense complexities, intense simplicities emerge.' –Winston Churchill

PAUL KEATING AND BILL KELTY WERE AN ODD COUPLE. If Keating evoked a latter-day Rudolph Valentino, then Bill Kelty, secretary of the ACTU, looked like Mickey Rooney playing a tough Irish kid in the movie *Boys Town*. Throughout the 1980s they were often seen together—Paul togged out in a Zegna suit, Bill in jeans and an Essendon football club T-shirt. What drew them together was their mutual interest in advancing social economics.

In the unionist, Keating found a legitimate Labor sounding board for his economic ideas. Kelty had a good degree in economics and, unlike most economists, a knockabout Irish-Australian personality. The two of them had lovely times together building up economic hypotheses without guile or restraint, on scraps of paper and on backs of cigarette packets—like two characters out of a Sean O'Casey play endeavouring to establish the validity of the immaculate conception. Keating's hypotheses, Kelty, with his classical economics training, might ultimately endorse or knock down. Keating did not mind, so long as they advanced. It was in this fashion that they workshopped universal industry superannuation.

There are two versions of how the industry superannuation funds got going. One holds that Paul Keating saw the futility of endeavouring to build a savings vehicle for the Australian worker based on lump-sum payments. How many Australian workers were going to grind towards a lump sum which, if it grew large enough, might disqualify them from the pension, and if it was small would most likely result in a pathetic spending splurge at the onset of retirement? With this insight, Keating took to Kelty the idea of building an annuity—a regular annual income—to take the place of a wage for workers once they retired.

The other version is that Kelty saw Keating fiddling with the taxation treatment of lump-sum pension payments, and went to him demanding that the lump-sum payment for workers be dropped and replaced by an annuity system built on pension funds set up within employee awards and financed by a mix of worker, employer, and government contributions. Whichever version is correct matters little; both endorsed the idea with enthusiasm and, in a spirit of Falstaffian good cheer, set out on a joint path to develop the industry-fund concept.

It was Keating who got the greater benefit from this relationship because of his capacity to seize upon an economic variable and build it into an engineering metaphor, like the revolving metal cylinders his father had made as an essential working part for ready-mixed concrete machines.

To Keating came the concept of savings, not as most people conceive it—putting away small amounts to build a nest egg—but as the relationship between national income and national spending. What matters in sweeping strategic terms is whether aggregate national expenditure—whether on shoes, homes, schools, freeways, steel mills, or atom-splitters—exceeds national income. The outcome for the nation must be a condition of either nett saving or nett spending.

It is possible for a nation to have a budget surplus while, overall, being in deficit because, in external terms, national expenditure exceeds income; this has, in fact, been Australia's general situation for many years. From Bill Kelty and then from the less unconventional Dr Chris Higgins, Bernie Fraser, Ted Evans, Don Russell, and other advisors, Keating learned that in dynamic, causative terms what mattered most in an external deficit was not really how much wool and wheat and iron ore you exported but, instead, factors to do with your propensity, as a community, to spend in excess of your income. And if this propensity was high, as it generally was in Australia, the ways of limiting it were few—as we are once again discovering. One could raise taxes so high that spending propensity was curbed, but this would kill economic endeavour. In a genuine democracy, this is politically unacceptable as a long-term strategy.

Keating saw that if every unionist in this highly unionised country agreed to forego some spending money and divert it into pension funds run by the unions, the scope for increasing savings in a dynamic sense was greatly enhanced. In 1984, Keating and Kelty set about convincing the Australian union leadership that it was a good idea to do this. The union bosses were far from a pushover, however, for a number of reasons. Some union leaders felt a powerful antipathy towards Paul Keating: he wore fancy foreign suits and, in becoming treasurer in the new Labor government, he had displaced their favourite son, Ralph Willis, a former ACTU advocate. Furthermore, they disapproved of Keating's initial action to reduce tax incentives directed towards building up pension lump sums. The basis of their objection to this change in tax incentives was ludicrous: a union member's lump sum relative to the lump sum that could be built up by a rich man was trifling. But union leaders didn't think in relativities; they didn't think beyond their own pockets in such matters. Finally, they disapproved of working people being told whether to spend or save their money.

Unless this union hostility could be reversed, Keating's whole concept of radical financial change throughout the 1980s and 1990s faced implosion because, unless the growth in savings—and therefore in financial capital—continued to accelerate, Macquarie and institutions like it could not manage to sustain the momentum of the growth in their overseas operations, and Keating wanted these as a new Australian industry.

Bill Kelty assembled—and ultimately converted—a group of key unionists nominated by the ACTU to go through this exotic proposition on superannuation. Within the group was Kelty himself; Garry Weaven from the Municipal Officers' Association; Simon Crean, then from the Storemen and Packers' Union; Martin Ferguson from the Miscellaneous Workers' Union; Laurie Carmichael, from the Metal Workers' Union; and Charlie Fitzgibbon, from the Waterside Workers' Federation.

'What in God's name have we got going on here?' union leadership asked. 'We're back in power, and the first thing we do is start taking money off workers for some bastard offspring of the institutions of capitalism.' Many in the union movement saw this as an ominous sign of instability, redolent of the

Whitlam government. Their reaction was not to consider it seriously, but rather to get whatever they could while another unstable Labor government ran its course.

The reference group worked for months until all were converted by the arguments of Kelty and Weaven; Carmichael not only came around, but played the group's intercessor with the left. A journalist covering the ACTU recalls waiting through one freezing September night in 1985 into the early hours of the morning until the group settled the provisions on portability and Kelty emerged to announce the endorsement of a workers' pension scheme. Industry-specific funds would be sponsored by their relevant unions in negotiations with employers, and the new arrangements involving employer contributions would be written into awards. A week later, the ACTU Congress met in Sydney and adopted the scheme, agreeing that an initial 3 per cent employer contribution should go to super in lieu of immediately spendable wage increases. The quarantining of these funds would serve as a major disinflationary step in the new government–ACTU accord.

Out of this pension-fund work emerged a grand advance in Keating's dynamic conception of Australia. The tripod would be history, to be replaced by what he was to call the golden circle. This, Keating subsequently explained to me, would be a line running through rising household savings, to rising capital supply, to rising international strength, to stable interest rates, and back to rising household net wealth.

A 3 per cent compulsory contribution to super was not nearly enough, either to provide adequate living conditions for elderly Australians or to fund the growing export in infrastructure and financial services, but it was a start. The following year, Keating put the industry pension funds into Commonwealth government legislation with a flexible regimen of rising contributions from workers, employers, and government. Underlying the legislation was Keating's timetable: by the year 2000, 15 per cent of workers' wages were to be compulsorily contributed to super. This target was not reached, because when the coalition was re-elected in 1996 it declined to raise the contribution beyond 9 per cent. Even at 9 per cent, however, the workers' funds in total amount now to $1 trillion. Keating says it should have been closer to $1.5 trillion by now, had the coalition continued the scheme.

A TELLING ARGUMENT within the ACTU reference group, when it put together the final recommendation to proceed with the Keating–Kelty superannuation funds as part of regular pay-and-conditions negotiations with employers, was the fees charged by traditional superannuation providers. When it explored possible superannuation arrangements, the union group found that the commercial superannuation industry—the traditional banks, AMP, Colonial Mutual, and so on—charged an average of 4 per cent-plus in fees. On this basis, the union group took the view that the unions could do without their services. They would be better off developing their own superannuation management. At this, they were very successful. Out of the unions' go-it-alone conclusions on workers' superannuation evolved a phalanx of men and women successfully managing multimillion dollar funds—in some cases, billion-dollar funds (the largest in 2007 was in charge of $22 billion). And out of this has emerged a new breadth and depth of expertise in the Australian workforce to match the explosion of talent and expertise in Macquarie Group and other financial institutions.

Garry Weaven epitomises the skill and initiative that has evolved since the superannuation agreements were struck. He has progressed through the funds-management business to a point where he now runs a business providing advisory and management services specialising in 'industry funds' as distinct from 'retail funds' (the commercial funds managers, AMP, Colonial, and so on). A distinguishing feature of Weaven's industry funds is that they seek no sales commissions, which makes a big difference to workers' ultimate receipts.

Income or commercial funds are those promoted by the salesmen and other representatives—accountancy firms, financial advisors—of the traditional providers of superannuation mentioned above. It is a matter of basic commercial importance to the commercial enterprises, such as AMP, BT, and Colonial, who manufacture and sell superannuation, that their representatives get their commissions. So the paying of commissions (upfront, ongoing or trailing) by the superannuating to the sellers is what distinguishes the so-called income or commercial funds from the industry funds.

In contrast, the industry funds sellers are motivated more by religion than by commerce. The industry funds are the children of the revolution; they are what came out of those nights of shoving and sifting by the original ACTU group. While the so-called industry funds were confined to the unions, the AMPs and Colonials were not greatly worried: it was unlikely that the unions were going to place their superannuation plans in the hands of the big end of town in any event. Nor were they particularly worried when the Labor government of the late 1980s and 1990s entered the lists by enshrining the industry funds in legislation which more or less compelled employer contributions in lieu of wage concessions into the funds in collective bargaining with the unions, and then brought in the government itself as a direct player by having it pay tax cuts into superannuation rather than as cash in hand.

Once the government came in with this sort of gambit, the traditionals saw that the government would have no option but to spread the industry funds beyond the unions: you couldn't have some workers receiving tax cuts direct and others receiving them by way of superannuation contributions. So the income funds, or commercial funds, drew the reasonable conclusion that once these industry funds got outside the complete grasp of the unions, they would have to enter the organising hands of the employer. And once they did, the employers would turn to the people they knew and trusted, namely the AMPs, Colonials, and the banks. The superannuation experiment would quickly turn at the margin to the advantage of the traditional providers.

By the 1990s, the industry funds had become not just a success but a galloping success. And as a result of the Keating government legislation, there were now three sorts of industry funds: those controlled wholly by the unions; industry funds in which the unions and the employers might share control; and industry funds run by employers and workers who lay outside the union movement. Among those outside the unions—the new industry funds in which the employers had as much, or more, say in the running of the operation as the workers—preference for the traditional commercial providers should naturally occur, the traditionals surmised.

But things did not go their way as much as they expected. For the traditional commercial superannuation providers, this was now a serious challenge. They assumed that employer-dominated funds that did not turn to the traditional providers must be under union duress, despite the ostensible employer hegemony. Once Labor was out of power, this situation required political lobbying to change the rules, to ensure that employers were perfectly free—more than free, if possible—to have the fund type of their choice and not one presumably foisted upon them by unions operating in the background. Free to choose, surely the employers would choose those financial institutions they had dealt with for years on other matters—on insurance, banking, mortgages and the like?

To the mortification of the old-line sales teams, it didn't happen that way; or at least it did not happen often enough. Take, for example, the MTAA Superannuation Fund that covers all Australian automotive dealers and members of the Automobile Chambers of Commerce, a body whose embrace extends as far as smash repairers. This is an umbrella group that covers everyone who sells cars and services cars after they are sold—people from major dealers to car salesmen, through to a variety of different tradesmen. The MTAA didn't go to the commercial funds.

The MTAA group covers 1100 businesses and 250,000 employees, and turns over $113 billion a year. It is an area of Australian business that would have been made for the traditional superannuation providers. But when the Labor government legislated for occupational superannuation in 1989, the MTAA elected to become an industry fund operating without the benefit of the commercials. It set up around it a new infrastructure in which it chose entities such as Access Economics, capable of casting fresh eyes over the business of portfolio strategy and portfolio selection. It began with a $5 million body of funds, and by 2006 it had $4 billion in its superannuation funds. Part of this growth is due to the expansion of employers and others under its umbrella. But it is nevertheless remarkable because it also grew rapidly through good management. And why should it now change from what the independent industry-fund structure has created to the traditional camp?

This was anathema to the traditional commercial institutions. The competitive friction between the commercial superannuation funds and industry superannuation still has a long way to run. There are parallels in the relationship between the big commercial banks of the 1970s and the unlicensed merchant banks and investment banks of the same period—of which Hill Samuel, the forerunner to Macquarie Group, was a prime example. The two breeds of super funds are rivals for the hearts and minds of employees and employers.

Just as the licensed banks were the establishment, ensconced in Paul Keating's tripod and encouraging dutiful respectability and conservatism above all else among their young, and the unlicensed banks were the new kids in town, so the AMP Society, Colonial Mutual Life, Mutual Life and Citizens, and National Mutual Life were part of a century-old group of providers of life insurance and superannuation services. While they lacked the protected status of the four commercial banks, nevertheless they saw themselves as part of the financial establishment. To them, the industry funds—or what they and John Howard preferred to call the union funds—were interlopers of an increasingly distasteful mien.

The differing natures of the people involved help explain the divisions. Those running the establishment savings houses tended to be conventional folk, often educated in the private school system, who might have joined their bank or 'life office' after their leaving certificate at, say, seventeen if they were male, and after their intermediate certificate at fifteen if they were female. And thus they progressed through their institutions, providing a valuable and thoroughly proper service to Australians while looking after their sales forces, who tended to be male and to have excelled at rugby or Australian Rules, or cricket or tennis—the kind of people who would be welcome among those seeking to establish superannuation schemes.

The industry-funds people are different. Most have had post-secondary education, but they have also worked in other employment; their ranks include former shearers, skin-divers, spray-painters, political advisors, journalists, and actors.

Michael Delaney, the man who runs the MTAA Superannuation Fund, is the very model of the modern major industry fund honcho; he had considerable exposure to politics and economics as an advisor to Gough Whitlam and then, surviving that, as principal private secretary to John Dawkins. Likewise, Gerard Noonan, the 2006 superannuation fund trustee of the year, fits the qualifications sketched above, and can articulate the social, political, and economic issues peculiar to this industry-fund personality as distinct from that of the commercial fund. This focus is important because political and financial rivalry between the two types is going to feature increasingly in the future.

I spoke to Gerard Noonan in 2007, before that year's general election. Noonan, a graduate of La Trobe University, described himself as the type of journalist who in the 1980s thought he was going to live forever and therefore had no need for superannuation. As a type, journalists were notorious for quickly spending everything they received and for going into debt to dubious sources in order to gamble on horses or cards. If there was any truth in Keating's somewhat paranoid belief that the Liberals didn't want to see the development of industry funds because workers had no business managing money, then, in the minds of the media owners of the day, journalists epitomised this type.

There was a small industry fund begun by the journalists and their union, and chaired by a senior Victorian journalist, Ian Baker. After Gerard Noonan became editor of the *Australian Financial Review*, he was approached by the secretary of the Australian Journalists' Association, Chris Warren, to see if he would consider taking its chair to replace Baker, who had gone into state politics. Thinking about it, Noonan could see that chairing such a fund was a job which, if done properly, was not dissimilar to editing a paper like the *Australian Financial Review*: it involved the consideration of social, political, financial, and economic issues at a high level. Noonan accepted the position, and has remained chair of the JUST industry fund ever since.

Not long after he took up the position at the relatively young age of 40, he received a sharp personal reminder of the relevance of superannuation. Conrad Black, a Canadian entrepreneur, had, through a company he controlled, taken a 25 per cent interest in John Fairfax and Sons, the Australian company that controlled the *Australian Financial Review*. Noonan, thinking that readers of the *AFR* would like to know something about their new absentee landlord, assigned three senior writers to do a profile on Black.

For the first time anywhere, the three *AFR* writers outlined how Black, controller of the London *Daily Telegraph* and other internationally prestigious media assets, was up-streaming income from his publicly listed media assets to a private company in Canada. Learning of this, Black arrived like an enraged bear in Noonan's office, demanding to know what he thought he was doing. Noonan explained a longstanding

Fairfax tradition of having their readers know something of their owners. This was of no avail. Black sacked Noonan, who repaired to Balmain to consider his future.

(In 2005, US attorney Patrick Fitzgerald brought eleven criminal fraud charges against Black and three former Hollinger executives in relation to their American activities. Black was found guilty on several counts of fraud, and sentenced to six years' jail, which he was expected to appeal.) It became a badge of honour for Gerard Noonan that he had refused to give an inch on the Black articles, and that after some weeks of bombast Black had fired him. 'It seemed bleak at the time,' Gerard Noonan says, 'but now I wear the badge proudly.'

Once sacked, he set up his own business from his home in Balmain and continued as chair of the journalists' and actors' fund. He was to return to Fairfax later as a senior editor on the *Sydney Morning Herald*. Through the years, he has combined full-time work as an editor-journalist with chairmanship of JUST. He was right, he says, in seeing an intriguing parallel between the role of an editor and the responsibilities one faces as the chair of an industry fund. He has never wanted to drop one in favour of the other, even though he is presiding over a corpus of fund money approaching a billion dollars and growing at 10 per cent a year. The synergy is there in his joint roles and, although the work gets onerous, he finds great satisfaction in the sight of journalists, actors, and other creative industry workers who are now part of the fund sitting on top of a billion dollars.

'When I first took on the chair we had $6 million, and I remember looking at the figure and thinking this is incredible; I can't even imagine what $6 million would look like,' he said. 'Now it's approaching a billion, I just feel the same. The board and I now have some 23 different fund managers investing across all of the asset classes, across the major markets of the world.'

'And you don't feel the need to devote yourself wholly now to what this entails?' I asked.

'No. I took the view some time ago that one must be careful of being mesmerised by the hugeness of what one is dealing with. One must be careful not to be intimidated by the priesthood of superannuation. There is out there in the commercial world of superannuation a body of people intent on creating the impression that they and only they are the high priests of superannuation investment. This is sheer posturing.

'I have found that if one keeps one's head and approaches this as one would the profession of editorship, one can proceed quite well: you decide upon a strategic allocation of your assets and you decide upon the different forms of investing needed to achieve this allocation, and as you go you get a handle on the terminology and you realise that a lot of this is part of the high-priesthood stuff that any religion uses. You come to realise that underneath the jargon are reasonably straightforward concepts that an intelligent person can grasp without too much difficulty.

'I notice that when we have a new board member, for about the first three months they are completely bamboozled by all this. So I always ease the new board members into the process. First up, I say, don't worry about a thing; it seems confusing now, but I can tell you it is straightforward: you've only got to apply common sense and you'll be a great board member. And that's what most of them have done. They have cut through the mumbo jumbo that masks the proposition that there are only a certain number of people who can actually invest.

'The end result is that AMP and Westpac funds management and the other commercial superannuation investors have to disguise their fee structure because they are only doing what we are doing, and they are charging a fee for it. We say we don't have to pay a fee to these people because you—the commercial funds—are just doing what we're doing and we can actually outperform you.

'What I've seen over the years in journalism tells me that you must be very careful in measuring capabilities by money payments. There are some complete dills running around earning millions of dollars.'

Gerard Noonan is a product of a blossoming of talent in Australian financial and political journalism during the past 30 years that parallels the change in the financial industries. This new journalism was unleashed in the 1970s by Max Newton, a former editor of the *Australian Financial Review,* who sponsored an elite strand of business, financial, and political journalists, often university-educated but also schooled by their rough-and-tumble experience in the news business. They were a new fourth estate, and part of the challenge to the financial and political establishment.

The financial institutions of the tripod are not going to lie down, the commercial superannuation houses no more than the four-pillar banks. So one can foresee a political struggle here between the old and the new that neither of the two main political forces have yet grasped.

I said to Gerard Noonan: 'It seems to me that the traditional super provider would have been better off without the evolution of the industry fund. So you must now expect the traditional fund to fight you politically, and by using public relations, every step of the way against expansion of the industry-fund system.'

'We not only expect it—we already see it,' he answered. 'In the case of AMP, they were caught out recently giving supposedly independent advice to fund clients, telling them to only go to AMP; they tried to harness for their purposes a conservative government's antipathy towards the industry funds.

'Clearly, the traditional funds like AMP have found the industry funds too hot to handle, in part because we have exposed the myth that there is something special about the AMP-type funds.'

I went on: 'Do you feel then that this AMP-type antipathy to the industry funds is a factor in the Howard–Costello government keeping the workers' contribution to superannuation at 9 per cent?'

'Absolutely. In view of what's happening, we are going to have to mount another campaign in favour of getting the move going again, towards first 12 per cent and then 15 per cent.'

Noonan pointed out that both the Coalition and the ALP had accepted 15 per cent as the benchmark employer contribution for politicians' superannuation: 'Howard and Costello deliberately turned off the tap at 9 per cent for ordinary workers, but have now presided over installing the benefits of a 15 per cent superannuation for themselves and other parliamentarians. We are going to have to revive the campaign for Keating's original timetable, to be approached in steps.'

Gerard Noonan is intellect working at the coalface of a new financial industry that Howard and Costello grasped poorly, if at all. Perhaps it is as simple as Keating says: Howard and Costello had a fundamental prejudice against the idea of unions running things as important as big finance. Keating offers the view that, in the eyes of Howard–Costello, you need a Liberal

Party ticket in your pocket for this job. Surely not? The number of fools in different guises on either side is substantial and about equal.

Whatever their reasons, Howard and Costello erred in snubbing the industrial funds: they should have used them as Keating intended to use them, as levers available in Australia, but not available in Europe and America, for exercising financial policy, in particular to encourage lower consumption and greater saving in times of pressure, to pull more private-sector spending back from spilling abroad. For it is now clear that the problems of excessive overall spending, in the private and public sectors combined—in an economic sense, the problems of insufficient overall saving—are far greater than John Howard and Peter Costello comprehended back in their salad days of government.

Chapter 6

The Antipodean Rialto

> 'The only sage advice I ever saw was that of J. P. Morgan who, when asked his secret, said, "The market will fluctuate."' –John Clarke

PAUL KEATING AND GERARD NOONAN ARE MATES. PAUL KEATING and David Clarke are not mates. Clarke is a private man who moves in circles where the appellation 'mate' is not often used. Nevertheless, when the history of Australia in the late 20th century is written, they will find themselves bound together: David Clarke as the founder of Macquarie Group, and Paul Keating as the man who signed the licence and whose policies opened the way for an international financial institution to emerge from Australia.

This is not to suggest that Keating went out of his way to help Macquarie Group in particular. The two are chalk and cheese: Keating is Eire Catholic, and Macquarie, in character, is Ulster Presbyterian. My point is, rather, that once having established the conditions for institutional change, Keating needed someone to show what could be done with the change, and it was Macquarie that was able to do that.

Neither Keating nor Macquarie would see Keating as a sponsor of Macquarie. Each would turn up their nose at the thought. But there is a divinity that shapes our ends, rough-hew them how we may. And I do argue that Clarke owes Macquarie's life to Keating, rather than to his friend John Howard. In turn, Keating owes a debt to Clarke and his colleagues for demonstrating what could be achieved once Australia was freed from the bonds of the national economic and financial regime that existed up until the early 1980s.

This is not a touting service. Like Keating's, my own interest in Macquarie is academic. Macquarie is used here as an example because its founders and their energies provide a model that sits very nicely on the side of my story that discusses the juxtaposed streams of politics and the market place. Within this confluence, great structural changes were being made, and great draughts of capital were being drawn from the pension funds. So it is fitting that the progress of Keating and of Macquarie are viewed in tandem. While Paul Keating was preparing himself for a Napoleonic political role, Macquarie was trying itself out in the financial provinces. The bank was positioning itself to move out into the world league, at a time when Keating's building work required a matching vehicle. Though Keating never defined it as such, Macquarie became a laboratory for testing how far his political mix could take Australia from being a backwoods amateur to a top international player.

The two simultaneous kinds of change—in political approach and in the market place—were both bred on an Antipodean Rialto, with an affinity that is exciting to see. Each is a fertile field on which to appreciate the development of human endeavour and folly. We see boldness, greatness, frailty, and delusion, and meanness and Iago-like jealousy. At full tilt, the streams of politics and market finance running together provide us with a spectrum not often seen elsewhere in human experience: of excitement and exhilaration, grace under fire, fear and greed, vast over-confidence and self-loathing, panic, scorn for those who fail in their advice, and deep remorse for having listened to the advice-givers in the first place.

Macquarie took up the money that the Keating–Kelty pension funds had garnered, and provided a return and financial rationale for those funds that was hard to fault for years. Macquarie put together packages of toll roads, power stations, and by-passes with assets that were semi-governmental in quality, and gave the nascent pension-fund managers the financial returns and peace of mind that were essential to allow this extraordinary Australian movement to get into its stride.

For twenty years, Macquarie voyaged with great winds gusting behind it. Its earnings per share seemed set fair to double every seven or eight years as it covered the globe with ventures in financial engineering: 33 per cent of its assets were in the UK and Europe, 41 per cent in North America, 26 per cent in Australia, and the rest largely in Asia. To have joined up early as an Australian shareholder, as the earliest pension funds did, was a euphoric experience. The share price doubled and appeared to be heading towards tripling. Even as late as 2006, Macquarie looked unstoppable.

But instead of breaching the $100 mark, as predicted, the wind in Macquarie's sails dropped drastically in 2007, falling 40 per cent through 2007 and into 2008, and then dropping further to 50 per cent from its peak in the autumn of 2008. There was only the nastier side of the human comedy in store for those who bought at $91 in early 2007 and sat through the air pockets to see it at $44 in March 2008. The buffeting followed

Macquarie's move away from putting together consortiums to build infrastructure and floating the resultant entity as a stand-alone enterprise on the share market, which had been a relatively simple process. The share-price drop is the result of moving into more complex, highly geared market products in cleverly built containers.

Between 2007 and 2008, Macquarie has illustrated the aforementioned frailties. In warfare and in a stock-market retreat, one sees humanity at its worst. In warfare, cruelty and official incompetence hold sway; in a stock-market retreat, an age-old human irrationality is on display, where the elements of logic embodied in such things as a share's price-to-earnings ratio count for very little. Mindless, atavistic fear takes over. There is no point in railing against this; atavistic fear in times of stress has been a predominant part of market behaviour since the Dutch Tulip crash of 1637, and no doubt long before then.

These behaviours repeat themselves down the generations, no matter how much learned research goes into explaining the share market. But as well as this general and apparently timeless phenomenon of share-market mindlessness, there is another aspect to the recent Macquarie share-price tumble which indicates that Macquarie shareholders could have been much worse off than they are at the time of writing.

This has to do with the contemporary behaviour of one set of financial players who have created a particular resonance in the story told in this book. Anyone following Australia's economic path during the past 20 years and contemplating it for the foreseeable future needs to gain familiarity with a set of institutions that are outside the control of the market or economic governance, whether national or international.

These are the so-called hedge funds, which believe that

they can make more money for their subscribers by operating as ruthlessly as possible outside conventional market rules. Their particular relevance to this story stems from the fact that they operate most effectively when they can isolate a target for attack. In the next chapter we will see how they operated in our region by isolating economies and attacking their currencies, and how the Keating reforms, by allowing new private-sector operations to quickly build a capacity for international currency-trading, allowed Australia to thwart the hedge funds in a way that Thailand and Indonesia could not. We will see how that currency-trading capacity saved Australia from the most fearful damage by shifting the battle for the Australian dollar in the 1990s into a wholly articulated international market rather than within the domestic market.

That is part of the adventure to come. Here we are looking at a narrower game. It is worth noting at this point, however, that the hedge funds appear to have lost their taste for taking on the Australian currency as a whole. Their memory of being bloodied in attacking Australia is still too recent. But they do have a taste for isolating and attacking certain Australian shares. These are shares which, in 2007 in one way or another, stood out from the pack. Macquarie qualified par excellence for this criterion. After growing so suddenly and swiftly out of the Antipodes, it has become an international investment bank, but one that can be made to appear to have no business being on the world stage.

There are also other factors that make Macquarie suitable for hedge fund attention. Since its early days, the bank has been the subject of one of the less attractive Australian characteristics, namely the tall poppy syndrome. Macquarie is young enough to have a considerable number of people in the investment industry—competitors, brokers, bankers, investment strategists, press commentators—who were there at the beginning when David Clarke and his colleagues embarked on their adventure. As Macquarie went from strength to strength in Australia, its success almost automatically generated jaundiced views of its quality, and heightened views of its vulnerability.

The hedge funds thrive on this. In the days when they were assailing the Australian dollar, they would dredge up stories of Australian political instability. One would find stories in the international press of a new opposition plot to block supply in the Australian Senate. As a preliminary to the more recent share assaults, Macquarie's errors and misdemeanours were highlighted in preparation for a strike. This behaviour is inherent to the nature of the hedge funds. They are run by people who sit in New York, London, Zurich, and Frankfurt, offering to make consistently larger returns for wealthy private investors than the investors could make if they put their money in conventional markets controlled by national and international authorities. To do this, the hedge funds must choose victims and exploit them.

The hedge funds are able to assemble huge bundles of liquidity, but to continue doing this they must demonstrate that they are more ruthless than conventional fund managers—faster on their feet and cleverer than people in ordinary stock markets, money markets, commodity markets, and in currency and share raids—and able to isolate victims like a lion isolates a gazelle. Their first step in doing this is to pick a currency or decent-sized share that looks vulnerable. They then spread stories about its weaknesses to make it look even more vulnerable, as they did with the Australian Senate stories in the days of the dollar attacks.

A tough hedge fund manager will bide his time, waiting for the right opportunity to add his voice to market fears. Thus, in late May 2007 at a symposium in San Francisco, Jim Chanos, a hedge fund operator who prefers to call himself 'a short seller', when asked to indicate the internationally operating share most likely to fall, nominated Macquarie. It is in this kind of situation that a hedge fund practises its art. The hedge fund operator begins by offering for sale shares the fund does not have in the knowledge that when the time comes to deliver such shares to the buyer, the operator will be able obtain them at a price lower than they sold them for, thus scoring an instant profit.

In the right climate, huge profits can be made in this way. Once the share price starts dropping, the operator repeats the exercise—selling shares he doesn't have, letting the market price fall further than the original sale price, borrowing the funds to acquire them, and then delivering them for real money. With anything—shares, commodities, currencies—the trick is to know when they are going to bottom out. The operator must not be caught out having to buy the shares at a price higher than he sold them for.

The trajectory of Macquarie's market performance in 2007–2008 is not pleasing: first it fell from $91 early in the year to $64 six weeks later, then there was a heartening recovery through the middle of 2007 up to $86, and then in the new year it fell again to $44. One has to try to put oneself in the position of the hedge fund traders. Did they stop short selling around $64 and let the price build up to the point where they thought that another bout of short-selling was in order? If a pattern like this were to recur it would be bad news for what is still an apparently strong stock on fundamentals. Such a pattern of falls and rises would begin to raise doubts about the suitability of Australia for an international investment bank of this size, and that would be as tragic for Australia as it would be for the particular stock, for it is on this kind of enterprise that we must look to build a new industry.

So the great billowing out from the Rialto has, temporarily at least, given way to a period of serious luffing and flapping, working to keep the ship from overturning. A period of introspection is in order. The heart of the nagging and monstering that surrounds Macquarie lies in its progression from its original role as a collector of long-term capital to build toll ways and by-passes, and selling investments in them on the strength of the day-to-day, trip-to-trip tolling calculations—which stand alone in the market place—into the creator of more and more clever pieces of financial engineering that creates separate 'boxes' which can be worked on as appendages to Macquarie proper. These boxes are capable of holding everything from the Chicago Skyway to nursing homes; each Macquarie box is designed to be insulated from the Macquarie Group mothership and, more importantly, Macquarie Group is designed to be insulated from the box.

Each separate financial box is started when the bank buys an asset and prepares it for earnings. As a specific example, let's return to the Chicago Skyway, a US toll road. The Skyway is sold into a financial box for a modest profit, and this Chicago Skyway box pays Macquarie an ongoing management fee. The operators of this box are free to leverage their asset (that is, to borrow money to buy the asset), on terms that mean servicing the debt will cost less in interest than the revenue generated by the asset. The yield on the asset is 'leveraged' up. If considered warranted—in, for example, a period of high capital expenditure—the box is able to borrow from the mothership,

Macquarie Group, to pay dividends; and, apparently, it isn't unknown, for limited periods, that dividends exceed cash flow from the asset. The operators of the box are free to re-value their asset from time to time when they think it is worth more. They are fine to do all of this, so long as the cost of servicing the interest on the debt does not rise permanently above the revenue from their asset. It is the fear of this final possibility that is helping to feed the current uncertainties about the value of Macquarie.

In press commentary, one is made adequately aware of the severe critics of the Macquarie 'model', as sketched above. In a climate such the present one, it is difficult to know how far uncertainty about Macquarie goes beyond what is reasonable. I went in search of criticism and found it abundantly represented in an article by Bethany McLean in America's *Fortune* magazine in September 2007. McLean introduces us to Macquarie by saying up front that it is 'highly controversial' without coherently saying why this is so. She parades Jim Chanos again, who says that, instead of inventing a new way to finance infrastructure, Macquarie is 'engaging in an old-fashioned Ponzi scheme'.

McLean's article doesn't tell us what a Ponzi scheme is, but shareholders who take the trouble of finding out are likely to proceed into the article scared witless. According to Wikipedia, a Ponzi scheme is a fraudulent investment operation that involves paying abnormally high returns to investors out of the money paid in by subsequent investors, rather than from net revenues generated by any real business. It requires an ever-increasing flow of 'investment money' in order to keep the scheme going

The article makes no attempt to justify this smear. The

author ends this part of her report and introduces the next with the following throwaway line: 'So what does it mean if the financial structures underpinning Macquarie's assets are actually as unstable as the steel that supported the Interstate 35W bridge?' This refers to a bridge across the Mississippi River in Minnesota that collapsed in 2007, killing 13 people and injuring about 100 others. Not content with this portrayal, elsewhere she sees enough that is 'flammable' in Macquarie 'to make people bet that in a tough market, something, anything, will catch fire and set off a chain reaction'.

The author alleges that Macquarie has excessive debt while also telling us that there is no way to assess whether this is true. There is nothing in McLean's text to justify the stream of vicious hyperbole. The quotes she uses from Jim Chanos, chief of the hedge fund Kynikos Associates, are highly dubious. Chanos is part of a trade whose job it is to talk down market assets—shares, currencies, and commodities—and then to judge if the talk has weakened the price support enough to make it the right time to strike. For a magazine as venerable as *Fortune* to lend itself to this hedge fund mischief is unspeakable. The author, however, doesn't rest at being part of the sharpest end of today's capitalist game. Elsewhere in this polemic, she dabbles in American socialism. Apropos of Macquarie being a party in the privatisation of the Chicago Skyway, McLean has this to say: 'There is widespread resentment and cynicism about the notion of private companies making money off [that is, buying and developing] what has long been perceived as public property.' This, in a featured article by the editor-at-large of a magazine called *Fortune*, which has been for generations—since that icon of American enterprise Henry Luce started it in 1930—an emblem of American private-enterprise capitalism.

The souls who stuck with Macquarie as 2007 turned to 2008 can take some comfort: Macquarie Group has incurred a stream of gratuitous and unsubstantiated denigration from America sufficient to test it. If it was as flimsy and 'flammable' as the article has it, it would indeed have burned up by now in the international share market downturn.

The fact that it has come through as well as it has must be taken as a considerable plus. But the bank is still in the sights of the hedge funds and, as they presumably have done quite well short-selling it in the past two distinct downswings, they will probably strike again. There is a danger now that Macquarie will become a more volatile stock than it was; shareholders might need to be prepared for a more-or-less continual cyclical experience.

It is difficult to see how Macquarie can rid itself of the smears on its reputation and thus thwart the short-sellers. Currently, it is taking what immediate action it can. Because Macquarie, no less than any of the conventional banks, is tied to the poisoned pool of US dollar deposit funds, it has announced its retirement from mortgage lending. But, with increasing recklessness, short-sellers can give the impression that Macquarie is leveraged towards the point of extinction — a calculation achieved by taking all the debt in its stand-alone boxes and coming up with debt-to-capital ratios as high as 95 per cent. In fact, its gearing (its debt-to-assets ratio) is 58 per cent on average.

As I depart this area of the text, I am grateful to be able to fall back on a long-standing area of British reserve. Late in April 2008, the London *Economist* ran a special article on Macquarie Bank and proceeded with none of the exaggerated spleen of America's *Fortune* magazine. It began ominously enough: 'When the credit crunch hit last year, few outfits looked more vulnerable than Macquarie Group.' In support of this, it quietly acknowledged that there were many on Wall Street who simply refused to believe that something like Macquarie could emerge from Australia and survive. Then, weighing these things up, *The Economist* concluded, 'Long-term concerns over Macquarie's model are bound to persist for as long as the world is worried about financing, accounting, disclosure and complex financial structures.' None of this is going to shake Macquarie more than it has been shaken. I include it here largely to underscore the extraordinary international attention that Macquarie now attracts.

My concern, however, is not for Macquarie per se; I do not own and never have owned the share. My concern, rather, is with the part played by Macquarie in the Keating revolution; and, at least as important, the part that must be played by enterprises similar to Macquarie if the revolution is to be completed. Later in this book I will explore the likelihood of its completion in the foreseeable future.

If the Rudd government engineers industrial pension-fund contributions up from 9 per cent of incomes to an eventual 15 per cent, as I think we can be fairly certain it will, this will mean a huge and accelerating wave of new investment capital coming in to Australian markets in the years immediately ahead. And if this is to do more than just inflate market prices, creative new enterprises must appear. The place for them to do so is in international investment-banking based in Australia. We must take up the coming surge in new capital by converging the needs of super funds with the abilities of entrepreneurs, similar to that which prevailed in the late 1980s and 1990s.

Macquarie has shown the place for new enterprise in

international investment from an Australian base. But the more that the hedge funds succeed in manipulating the price of a Macquarie-type enterprise, the more difficult success will become for such enterprises. The more that the hedge funds succeed in their aims, the more the Australian enterprises will end up existing for the benefit of the manipulator rather than for the shareholders and their community. As the share is manipulated, the enterprise is checked and potentially destroyed. And this is before the longer-term uncertainties of a Venetian voyager can be known.

AT A POINT SUCH AS THIS, a fashionable current practice in social science and business analysis is to return to the past in seeking guidance for the future. For Australian investment banking there is a diverting reprise to be had—both in terms of states of origin and personality-types involved—from 19th-century Scotland. It is a reprise which demonstrates, given time, the irony of an enterprising life, in that Scotland lost the drive of its entrepreneurial vehicle not through any fault of its own but through the unknowable consequences of a great war.

In the last half of the 19th century the Scottish American Investment Company, financed initially by such entities as Scottish Widows, formed and began a spectacular career of investment banking, organising and financing infrastructure and real estate in North America. Through no fault of its own, the Scottish American eventually ran out of steam when it was required to sell its overseas investments and invest the proceeds in UK government debt to finance World War I—an event which had unforeseeable financial influence at least as great as its social, political, and territorial influence. Allowing for the great differences in development generally and information technology in particular between then and now, consider the following paradigm.

From the middle of the nineteenth century, London became the world's most powerful financial capital, and a feature of the British Empire was London's ability to fund the development of infrastructure throughout the empire. In fact, where capital was concerned, a fair amount of poetic licence was applied to what defined the British Empire. Places like Argentina were surreptitiously taken under its wing. However, the most important part of empire became those former rebellious colonies directly across the Atlantic. Directly and indirectly, London, after the American Civil War, became a major factor in the development of the Americans' railroad system which, in turn, became crucial to the development of the United States.

The London banks fed the great family fortunes of England and elsewhere into the development of North America. The Scottish fed in the 'many a mickle makes a muckle' savings of the lowland Presbyterian Scots. History knew little of the separate Scots contribution until two American scholars, Leonard Bushkoff and Saul Engelbourg, identified a man named John Stewart Kennedy who, in combination with the Scottish American Investment Company, led Scotland into a big role in American railroad building, particularly railroads west of the Mississippi, not unlike the way Macquarie Group is leading Australia out into the world. The parallel is a bit rough, but it is worth pursuing. Its relevance lies in the lesson of what a small country and enterprise can do, given discipline and coordination matched with drive in using a stream of savings beyond the immediate needs of the country itself.

Scotland's efforts were home-grown and, like Macquarie,

came from a small base. In the decade between 1873 and 1883, Scotland, then a country of about three million people, provided about two-thirds of total British investment in American railroads, through a combination of deftly managed American stock market securities and American mortgages, particularly those taken on western grazing lands beyond the Mississippi.

The Scots in their golden age assembled capital for America out of the remarkable saving urge of the country's middle and working classes. Australia, in the current age of overseas capital investment, enabled Macquarie Group to assemble funds from the machinery that Paul Keating and Bill Kelty put in place for the old-age comfort of a distinctly un-Presbyterian collection of Australian unionists, through the industry funds. The grassroots sources of investment were quite different, but the processes were largely the same: relative to the sizes of the countries, a huge flow of investment money came from armies of individuals willing to put their money in the conservative hands of people whom they knew and trusted.

The relatively small Scottish banks observed and learned from the experience of their London betters: the London banks lost (and gained) fortunes through channelling their funds into New York banks on the reasonable assumption that they would know better the traps in investing in the free-wheeling private sector of the United States. Too often, the trust of the London banks was misplaced, and the Scottish banks knew that the sensitivities of their smaller-scale individual investors would not be able to withstand major collapses in America that the better-bottomed London banks had endured along the way.

So the Scots went in quest of 'point men'—men on the spot, those rare birds who combined toughness and adventurism with honesty, integrity, loyalty, and acumen. Naturally enough, they went for young Scotsmen, not just because of national bias, but also because Scotland then had the best primary and secondary public education system in the world, proceeding through reading and writing and arithmetic to such things as bookkeeping and business studies.

The young Scots had to be travelled enough in America to understand the dangers of putting money into ventures in a no more than marginally governed land, where the laws and enforcements of state governments—in some contrast to the US federal government—were free and easy, and guided by the conclusion that if money had to be lost, it was best that the British were the first casualties, in preference to the natives.

The Scots were too late for the railway bonanzas in the eastern United States. The Scots' time was after the Civil War, and thus of necessity was more directed to the wild unknown that was the west. It was an economically perilous period. By the early 1870s far too much building activity and investment had occurred in the name of reconstruction. A deep and long construction recession set in that was like a minefield for players from over the water.

John Stewart Kennedy was one of nine children of a Scottish mill hand, a boy who rose through the Scottish education system and reached New York as the employee of a Glaswegian exporter of iron, a commodity in huge demand for the American railroads. He was picked out from the iron trade in New York by William John Menzies, founder and managing director of the Scottish American Investment Bank, headquartered in Edinburgh. Kennedy got the broad brief from Menzies that he was to 'purchase securities, to transmit them to us, to collect our coupons, and to advise us as to anything going on your side of which we ought to be aware'.

At the outset of a slide into depression there was a myriad of things going on his side, and Kennedy soon showed his value. With integrity in contrast to the Wall Street operators who passed the shares in about-to-fail railroads and other ventures to their friends in London, Kennedy watched and separated out the ventures that were going to fail from those that would scrape through. Kennedy collected for Menzies the bonds of those that were going to scrape through at deeply discounted prices, and thus got some splendid bargains. The Scottish bank not only survived the crash, but in the fullness of time profited very handsomely from it.

Thus began a 25-year relationship between Kennedy and the Scottish American Investment Bank, in which Kennedy rarely put a foot wrong. He was helped by canny Scottish investment rules, one of which was to diversify your portfolios. Scottish investment proclaimed that not more than one-tenth of capital was to be invested in any one security. These early years of informed picking of investments from the downs of the New York Stock Exchange explains why so much of this Scottish investment in railroads at this time went through stock exchange investments rather than direct ownership of the railroads. At a time when American railroad entrepreneurs were not averse to building a railway line alongside another company's line—to the accompaniment of gunfire and explosions—to ensure that the other company's line went bust, direct investment was a dangerous investment; better to have a shrewd head pick the eyes out of enterprises as they emerged on the Wall Street lists throughout the recurring share-market busts.

Kennedy gave his own advice to Scottish American before he bought shares himself. He advised in 1873 of an impending tumble on the New York Stock Exchange: his boss came straight across from Edinburgh and, four days later, J. Kay Cooke and Co., a substantial New York broker, went under and the market plummeted. It was the worst panic in American history to that point. As the year moved towards its end with market prices falling, Kennedy began buying heavily for the Scots, with Menzies looking on. Said Menzies, as older, better, established banks were broken by the panic: 'Not one security we have taken through Kennedy is in any way suspicious.' Kennedy's reputation blossomed. He and Menzies bought bonds in the Canada Southern Railway just as the panic began. By January 1875 the line had missed an interest payment, and the bank asked Kennedy if it should sell its holding. No, said Kennedy, hang on. The New York Vanderbilt interests shortly after bought in and brought new capital into the railroad. Canada Southern survived and prospered.

The panic eased and the cycle turned. Kennedy turned to personal involvement in re-organisation. From the wreckage of several western railroads, he and four others formed the St Paul, Minneapolis and Manitoba line, which became one of America's greatest trans-Mississippi lines, reaching the Pacific in 1893. Into this he brought the Scottish American. As the Manitoba began pushing across the great plains from Canada, it looked for a sustained source of long-term capital. The Scotsmen, who had begun their investment bank less than 20 years before by picking the eyes out of stocks on Wall Street, became one of the great cross-border capital suppliers, on the condition that Kennedy stayed to watch over their interests and see the Manitoba through, which he did, and handed it on as a major success.

Macquarie thus far has never had to deal with gunfire

through the campfire lights at night, or the dynamiting of bridges, as a rival consortium tried to parallel their freeways through Asia, Europe, and America. International law is much more stable today. But one can see the principle inherited here. Rather than sift through the *Financial Times* to find a toll road for sale, there are Macquarie point men (and women) all over the world ready to bring back to the Australian bank a proposal for investment in major infrastructure from ten thousand miles away. If it checks out, Macquarie will organise the capital and—to a degree that John Stewart Kennedy could not have conceived of—the detailed calculations of traffic density and toll charges necessary for it to get to the point where it can be taken for floating to world share markets.

There is a direct parallel in the case of the Manchester bypass, where a remarkably organised financial and structural operation from the relatively small country of Australia came in to take over a big project from a British consortium not coping with original plans. And by this time Macquarie had progressed and prospered sufficiently from the initial infrastructure projects in Australia to enable it to proceed without borrowing to meet its part in construction costs. Macquarie was sufficiently cashed-up to hold Manchester, which is one of the best motorways in the world, as a stand-alone project.

It is possible that Scotland would have ended up as the world's richest small nation had World War I not intervened; it suffered more than most other participants in that ghastly debacle. The Scots literally gave their life blood to the British crown: 74,000 out of a population of fewer than four million were killed in the conflict, and the country's capital and business initiative became barren servants of war. By the end of it, the enterprise, adventure, and drive that had characterised the activities of John Stewart Kennedy, William John Menzies, and others were washed out of the Scots for a generation or more.

The Scottish story is over; in the case of Australia, the story is still unfolding, and its denouement is a large part of what this book is about. Keating and Kelty knew that 9 per cent of workers' salaries for superannuation was a good effort, but it wasn't good enough. To complete the exercise they'd begun, and to leave Australia as a copper-bottomed world-beater in investment machinery, they needed to go on lifting the contribution to superannuation from workers' incomes to 15 per cent. Why the Howard–Costello combination cut it off at 9 per cent on their accession in 1996, and then let its potential for further build-up flow instead into such things as desultory, counter-productive, tax cuts is one of the mysteries to be pursued. Bemused international observers have said that the Howard government's action of cutting off the workers' superannuation build-up arbitrarily at 9 per cent is the strangest act on the part of a conservative government seen ever, anywhere in the world. More of this later.

BY THE TIME the chairman of Macquarie, David Clarke, and I met for lunch in 2006, he and his colleagues were a national and international success story and not yet bothered by the hedge funds. David was a presence of quiet reverence in the Australian Club. We sat under the overwhelming 1917 Arthur Streeton painting of Mount Buffalo, known in the club as *Blue Depths*—and aptly so, as a monumental gap in the Australian Alps leads indigo into blue and then into green in merging shades to a horizon far beyond.

With what I hoped was polite provocation, I began the

exchange: 'Without the things that Keating did—the bank competition legislation, the currency float, the removal of all those external regulations—Macquarie could not have risen from a three-man office to do the great things it has done.'

'If you say so, David,' said Clarke.

'It is a point I would assume people at Macquarie and those who imitate Macquarie would make, if only to themselves, when they hear Howard—as one frequently does these days—dismiss Keating as an irrelevance.'

'Does Howard do that?'

'He does. And don't you find it amazing how Howard can dismiss the playing field which Keating delivered him at change of office: the 1 per cent inflation rate, the period of 3 to 4 per cent a year productivity growth, 5 per cent wages growth, the forces turning the budget around to booming surplus. These were Keating's legacy to Howard, and Howard denies it.'

'What are you trying to do here, David, deny Howard any credit for the last ten years?' he said.

'No, I am not trying to deny him credit at all. What pisses me off, though, is that Howard thinks that he and his government have done it all. Without Keating he couldn't have done it.'

'I think you are not allowing John Howard enough credit here,' said Clarke. 'Between them, Keating and Howard provided for Australia an extraordinary 30 years of change. Both Keating and Howard contributed.'

'That's not what Howard says,' I countered.

'What he says and what he thinks is something we can't answer here.'

I felt myself checked. He hadn't come here to have an argument about Howard and Keating. I studied the Streeton briefly and looked back into his sandy, Scottish face. 'Apart from being very smart, David, what is there about Macquarie's operations that differentiate you from other enterprises?'

'Well,' he answered, 'one thing is that, apart from the very major decisions, such as the decision to seek a bank licence, we don't follow a policy of top-down in our operations. Among our professionals we follow a policy of from bottom up: the way is always open for someone, however young, to develop an idea and take it forward.

'For example, for some time before we became Macquarie Group we had an office in London, largely broking Australian equities to investors in London. Once we became a bank we sent some of our infrastructure people over to the office for experience. On their own initiative, it was they who scouted around England and came back to us with the plan for the Manchester bypass. It now stands as one of the few toll ways in the UK, and it works brilliantly. It became the overseas paradigm for the Macquarie Infrastructure Group, and helped establish a listed funds structure which is now in total something over $30 billion.

'The Manchester toll road became the model for the Macquarie Infrastructure Group's work around the world. We listed MIG on the stock exchange and were able to go to the market for funds while a major project like Manchester progressed. Then when Manchester was completed and bringing in its own revenue, it was able to become a source of operating cash flow for new projects like it elsewhere in the world. This became the pattern for us: do the project aided by cash flow from existing projects, then get it on to a good stock market and get it into one of the funds which can help for a time with another project of the same category.'

'So now it all just rolls on for you?'

'No, I wouldn't say that. This cross-city tunnel affair in Sydney, which we're not involved in, has done a fair bit of damage to public–private concepts in toll roads in particular, with a lot of governments. The concept is no longer the flavour of the month it once was.'

'But since the Manchester job and others like it, you must have moved up into a class of your own,' I said. 'If one concept ceases to be flavour of the month, you seem to find yourself just coming up with another. Looking back, you would appear to be a public relations operation's dream. Did you have PR people making sure the name Macquarie Group continuously appeared favourably in the *Financial Times*, the *Wall Street Journal* et al.?'

'No. We didn't go out of our way to court that sort of thing. Of course, we looked for good word of mouth about ourselves. But the one thing that made us breakfast table conversation across the world was quite unintended in that sense.'

'What was that?'

'That was our bid for the London Stock Exchange. We thought the institution fitted with us. You see, you can argue that the London Stock Exchange has a lot of the same characteristics as a Macquarie infrastructure project: it has monopoly status; it is regulated and has reasonably steady cash flows. Investors pay it a per-transaction fee like a toll road fee. It is quoted on its own stock exchange, just like the Australian Stock Exchange is quoted here. We did a lot of work on it and came to the conclusion that it was undervalued. We got a consortium together and put in a precise bid of £5.80 per share.'

'My God. One can imagine establishment people in boardrooms around the city biting the edges off tables at that one. Was there an outburst? "Who do these colonials think they are?"'

'There was some of that. But there was also a good deal of positive reaction. The market price of the Exchange immediately shot up way above our bid. The common view was that our bid was just an opening feeler, and that if we were serious we would go higher. But we'd done our sums carefully, and that's what we figured it was worth. Then the New York Nasdaq came in with a bid, and the price went even higher. I think it went up above £11; it became a worldwide thing. We didn't move our bid, because that's what we thought it was worth, and if we could have got it for that we would have taken it. It quickly became overpriced.'

'You got press comment all over the world.'

'We certainly did. Overnight, people across the world wanted to have a look at us. But we didn't do it for that.'

'Meanwhile, back to the grind, eh? You were talking about how you needed to develop concepts beyond the toll road infrastructure type of thing?'

'I would not say we were ceaselessly trying to come up with new concepts. But beyond Manchester our people looked out for new concepts. And we came up with an interesting distribution of things. In a couple of major international cities we have simply returned to the kind of concept we started off with in Hill Samuel days in Australia. Take Milan. All we are doing in Milan is mortgages, as we started all those years ago with Hill Samuel. Then, having successfully started that in Milan, we've moved into a mortgage business in Memphis, Tennessee. We identified in both America and Italy an opportunity to do the Australian-style mortgage exercise; that is, with securitisation—bundle the mortgages together and insure them with a top-quality insurer, and then create from that blue-chip investments. Where we see an opportunity to do something we have done well before, we will do it.'

'Do you look mainly now for those things based on property and infrastructure as the preferred course?'

'Not necessarily. We do what we think we can be good at. Where we have been good at something right from the early days—in Johannesburg, for example, we do a lot of bullion trading, and while we're there we're building up derivatives trading. In Abu Dhabi we've got a joint venture with a bank. Throughout South-East Asia we've got a lot of stock broking. We bought the old Barings securities business—we bought their stock broking business as ING with operations all over South-East Asia, and it has been a great acquisition. We have a real estate investment trust in Singapore with a diversified portfolio in business parks and science parks, high-tech industrial facilities, and distribution and logistic centres. In Korea, we have the Korean Opportunities Fund. Elsewhere in Asia, we have investments in warehousing and distribution in Hong Kong, cable television services in Taiwan.'

'Outside Asia, do you have diversification away from the traditional public–private infrastructure—away from the toll road model?'

'Of course. The Macquarie Airports Group covers airports all over the world. Macquarie Communications is invested in communications across the world. The Macquarie Leisure Trust invests in tourism and leisure widely. The Macquarie Media Group is invested in media assets globally. Macquarie Power invests in power in North America.'

'You moved from Manchester to toll roads in North America. Did that lead to this kind of diversification in the States?'

'Oh yes. The Macquarie DDR Trust has a portfolio of shopping centres all over America. Macquarie Countrywide invests in supermarkets all over America. The Macquarie Office Trust invests in commercial office property all over America. Macquarie Prologis has a portfolio of warehouses and distribution centres across the USA. Macquarie Parking has invested widely in off-airport parking. There's the individual Icon Parking, which handles most of the parking in New York.'

'What are the limits to your expansion? Obviously, not funds these days.'

'The biggest limit we've got is being able to attract the right people. We're fortunate being based in Australia, because I think the first preference of a young person wanting to get into investment banking is Macquarie Group. We're now getting around 60,000 applications a year for professional jobs here.'

'And with all your drive, how much of that application list can you take?'

'About 300 to 400.'

'Good God. Is that all? What happens to all the rest of that intelligence?'

'Well, being the right person for a job here is not just a matter of intelligence. The 60,000 gives us the luxury of a very big selection base. But we need all of that to get the right combination of talents. The process begins to sort itself out before we get to the point of telling young people we don't want them. Some find after exploration that it's not for them.'

'But even so, 60,000! You can discount that a lot and still say that something remarkable is going on here. What you're unearthing here is an enormous resource. What is this saying about Australia?'

'It's saying that we've got a very good professional workforce in Australia all round.'

'What's happening to those you don't take?'

'Well, there are people like Babcock and Brown, Goldman Sachs, and so on, now doing the same things as us from Australia. Some can go to them.'

'Yes, but if you only take 300 to 400, Babcock and Brown and Goldman Sachs aren't going to make that much of a hole in the 60,000.'

'Yes, well, looked at from a world viewpoint, it seems that Australia is a very good place for a financial services industry. Relative even to Wall Street, we are a very good producer and supplier of financial services.'

'And it's something that's happened so recently,' I said. 'Thirty years ago, we certainly weren't a very good supplier of financial services. We were among the worst.'

'Thirty years ago,' said Clarke, 'the industry simply didn't exist here. It's all happened since we started. We have gone from being one of the most regulated markets in the world to a very efficiently deregulated market.

'Australia is now a particularly good place for financial services. Australia has now got in place the legislative things needed for that. I was on a committee chaired by Nick Whitlam: to get a totally new legislative framework up for offshore banking facilities out of Australia. After some hard work, we got that. So we're now taking business away from Singapore and Hong Kong.'

'How does that operate?' I asked.

'It's for business that is completely offshore. But you do it through a structure which is like a branch of onshore operatives, where you only pay 10 per cent tax on your income. You don't start out doing it to encourage tax minimisation; you do it because if you didn't offer the service you would lose business on a wider base to Singapore and Hong Kong. It took a bit of time to get going. But now it's successful. The bureaucrats hate it; the politicians, though, actually like it. It is the one further string we needed for our bow.'

'I think there's a final barrier we have got to go through, David,' I said. 'And that's sustained life for all this financial enterprise activity under a Labor government, without Paul Keating. That old proto-communist element that entrenched itself through the war years and after, in the Labor Party and the unions, and then revived itself under Doc Evatt—it's still there underneath the surface. Keating held them at bay through Bill Kelty's influence with the unions. But if they got the kind of sway they had in the Whitlam government, all our incredible free market gains would be at risk.'

David Clarke said nothing. So after a short while examining *Blue Depths*, I felt a certain amount of interlocutor's declaration necessary: 'We have got to have lived through the experience of a Labor government in which we can be satisfied that the confused, union-dominated, Aussie version of Peronism has been removed, or sufficiently tamped down, before we can finally pronounce Australia an outstanding world success. This is the final test: to have a Labor government without destroying what Keating managed to build.'

David Clarke, wary of my attempts to have him declare himself on points of political philosophy, again said nothing. So I put it another way: 'I just can't see why, given worldly politics here, Australia cannot be a kind of Switzerland in cleverness and economics.'

This released Clarke: 'I agree with you. But I don't agree with what you seem to be implying on Keating versus Howard. I think both contributed greatly to an extraordinary 30 years, and Howard must not be dismissed in the way you are inclined to go. As to the Swiss analogy, I think that is apt. We have already gained a lot of that balance and efficiency under Howard. Indeed, I think we can be better than Switzerland in a lot of respects. I think we are going to have more drive and creativity, and financial services is leading to that.'

'And the 60,000 young people who identify themselves each year by applying to Macquarie Group?'

'Of course, they are part of it. It is our responsibility to advance as we have been advancing. Because we have made Australia a place of success for our kind of activity, there are more and more enterprises wanting to get going here. But you can't expect us to go out and set them up to compete with us just to accommodate the excess of young people who apply to us. There's plenty of competition developing here.'

'Is there a danger that we'll lose too many of these young people?'

'I don't think so. My experience is that Australians like living in Australia. Quite a few may go to New York or London for experience, but most of them will come back. Most of Macquarie's top people, and most of the top people of our competitors, could all earn a lot more money elsewhere. Despite the criticism within Australia of what we get paid, they could all earn a lot more money on Wall Street. If the main concern for them was chasing the almighty dollar, they'd all be over in Wall Street, London, or Hong Kong. But that hasn't proved to be the case.'

Chapter 7

Beating Off the Hedge Funds

'The Assyrian came down like a wolf on the fold,
And his cohorts were gleaming in purple and gold.'
–*The Destruction of Sennacherib*, Lord Byron

IN *THE BONFIRE OF THE VANITIES*, HIS NOVEL ABOUT WALL STREET in the 1980s, Tom Wolfe called investment bankers 'masters of the universe'. But as Philip Coggin, capital markets editor of *The Economist*, recently pointed out, that title now correctly belongs to the hedge fund managers. Hedge funds have been around for half a century, but their activity has grown aggressively in the past 20 years. In the 1990s, they almost destroyed some Asian economies and posed a serious threat to Australia's continued growth. That episode is worth revisiting, because it demonstrates how the economic reforms of the Hawke–Keating era underpinned our economic survival when the hedge funds attacked the Australian dollar. It also provides an insight into some of the problems we could face because those reforms have been allowed to stall.

In the early 1990s, our region of the world was notable for its arc of so-called Asian miracle economies—Thailand,

Malaysia, Indonesia, Singapore, the Philippines, and South Korea. By following the tutelage of the International Monetary Fund and of the USA's official agencies, these nations had transformed themselves into the fastest-growing economies in the world. They were international showpieces. The IMF liked to make the point that, by following a formula of openness to international investment, particularly in the export sector, they were setting an example to other developing economies, and that more developed economies like Australia's could take a leaf or two from their books.

These economies became so attractive to international investors, in particular the Japanese, that money poured into their property sectors as well as their export manufacturing bases, and these funds were husbanded into their international reserves rather than into inflationary current spending. The IMF prescription was followed to the letter, until something happened that signalled a souring of this idyllic economic performance: Alan Greenspan, then chairman of the US Federal Reserve, began to raise American interest rates to head off domestic inflation. In turn, the Japanese were forced to raise their rates to keep pace with the US. Above all, Japan needed to avoid a weakening of the yen, because a strong yen was the cornerstone of the buoyant Japanese economy.

With growing wealth, excellent credit access, and a notably low inflation rate at home, Japanese investors had looked around for markets outside Japan in which to invest some of their bounty. They focused first upon Thailand, where they saw the local business elite, formed by the integration and intermarriage of the Thai aristocracy with the Chinese merchant class, as a platform for creating a Japanese-funded export base that was cheaper and more competitive than their own. To secure Japanese investment, the Thai government tied the baht irrevocably to the US dollar. Between 1985 and 1992 the Japanese invested US$5.2 billion in Thailand, and the result was a dramatic surge in Thai exports.

Other South-East Asian economies proved almost as attractive to investors, but let us concentrate here on Thailand and Indonesia. The price of land in Thailand sky-rocketed as Japanese funds poured in. The rest of the world caught on; international developers arrived in droves, and property development boomed. Cranes rose on Bangkok's skyline, and Japanese golf courses sprang up across the lush Thai landscape.

The Thai miracle began to end when the Japanese authorities decided that the Japanese boom had to end, and proceeded to induce one of the most rapid escalations in monetary tightening anywhere in the past 30 years. It was 1989, and Japanese official interest rates shot up. Japanese asset values collapsed, and investors had to scramble for funds to cover these falling values. The Thai economy suffered collateral damage as Japanese investors liquidated their overseas assets. The Thai authorities scrambled into action, removing all constraints on capital inflow, while keeping the Thai baht fixed to the US dollar. They continually expanded the categories of banks and other international entities permitted to inject funds into the Thai economy for on-lending. At the same time, they raised interest rates competitively.

The government and the nation's international lenders continued to assure each other that Thailand was an Asian tiger par excellence. But the hedge funds saw something different—a sub-stratum of Japanese investors anxious to exit baht as quickly as they could to meet commitments back home in Japan. The short-selling of currency began. With borrowed US dollars, the hedge funds bought unofficially devalued assets and presented the baht proceeds at the official Thai window to receive more dollars than they had borrowed.

The process was similar to the sell-off of borrowed Macquarie Group shares described in the previous chapter, except that in this case the hedge funds didn't even have to worry about market fluctuations that they couldn't control, because the Thai central bank stood in the market as a stanchion day after day, paying out a fixed US-dollar price for baht. The nation's reserves fell, the Thai authorities could not keep up the relentless pace, and before long the system cracked. The value of the baht plummeted; and as interest rates were cranked up in an attempt to hold dollars in the country, they rose to a level that began to destroy assets in the real economy.

A month after the Thai collapse, the hedge funds turned on the Indonesian rupiah. The IMF came forward with US$23 billion to add to the $US20 billion that the Indonesians already had in reserves. But the momentum was too strong, and the defeat of Thailand too disillusioning, for Indonesia to bear. Among Indonesian companies and banks that had borrowed US dollars, fear spread quickly that the cost of repaying their loans would quickly become ruinous in rupiah terms. In the domestic economy, prices leapt under the pressure of the depreciating rupiah, and riots broke out as many Indonesians went hungry or lost their livelihoods. In Jakarta alone, 500 people died in the unrest. At the outbreak of the crisis, you could buy one US dollar for 2000 rupiahs. By the time the hedge funds had finished, the value of the US dollar was 18,000 rupiahs.

The hedge funds also had their eyes on Australia. They had little doubt that, once a couple of the Asian tigers had been knocked over, it would be profitable to turn on the Aussie dollar. We would weaken because of real economic changes in our region: the tigers had constituted the miraculous growth on which Australia was supposed to be reliant for her own economic expansion. Not only the hedge funds thought they saw this; our friends in North America and Europe thought they saw it, too, and they withheld investment funds from the Australian share market. Our economic vulnerability to the hedge funds was conventional wisdom at the time.

It is difficult to imagine the consequences if the hedge funds had succeeded here. It would have been a catastrophe, comparable in the imagination, say, to the impact on Britons if the German military had stepped across the Channel as they could have done in 1940.

For Australia, there would have been three stages of defeat: first, the funds would have driven down the Australian currency in the open market to a point where our own reserves and the reserves that the IMF and the US Fed could provide us with would have been exhausted, and we would have had to cease the free float of the dollar, re-imposing exchange controls and withdrawing the right to trade in the currency in the open market by anyone other than the central bank. With that, a central rationale for investment banks like Macquarie that operated internationally would have disappeared. For the commercial banks, the scope for real flexibility in deposit-raising would have gone. The ability of Australia to use the world as its palette for mixing investment flows around the world would have ended. Finally, we would have been forced back to a stultifying financial conservatism, and to the rationing of funds from a cautious and unimaginative central government. In other words, we would have returned to hick status.

As it turned out, the hedge funds went away from Australia with their noses bloodied. The fact that the 1990s hedge fund wars never seriously looked like ending with the worst-case scenario was a victory for Australian financial forces. The elements of the victory deserve closer analysis. Such an assessment is an exercise underrated by strategists and historians alike.

The source of Australia's success in seeing off the hedge funds lay back in the mid-1980s, in the early interaction of bold official financial reform and informed, imaginative private-sector responses. From the day the dollar was freed, David Clarke and his colleagues were on hand, knowing where to go to set up an open market in the Australian dollar vis-à-vis every other tradable currency in the world, quickly establishing depth and resilience in the market.

As the 1980s turned into the 1990s, there were two good reasons why there should be a substantial international market in the Australian currency. One was our location in a time zone that required Australia to be open when most of the trading world was closed. The other was that the international real asset investment activities of Macquarie Group, and those that shadowed it, were cashing US currency into Australian as a fundamental outgrowth from their business.

One of the reasons Clarke and his team had been anxious to shuck off Hill Samuel International was because the Hill Samuel parent had no desire to accommodate its Australian offspring's wish to get strongly into Australian dollar trading in New York. Once Hill Samuel Australia cut free of its parent, and the Australian dollar floated, the bank no longer faced constraints on its international trading. It set up its desks in London and New York, and got to it. By the time the international hedge funds came around our door, Macquarie Group was a well-established currency trader, and a significant market-maker in the Australian dollar.

When the hedge funds turned from the East Asian currencies to the Australian dollar, Bernie Fraser was head of Australia's central bank. Once the aggressors were identified, Fraser had his staff go through a checklist: first, was the Australian real exchange rate (the exchange rate adjusted for inflation differences between ourselves and our trading partners) overvalued? It was not, and thus, if it proved necessary, the Reserve Bank had to be prepared to mount the most vigorous defence it could against sustained speculation in the currency.

But what of the forward economy? At the time of the first hedge fund assault, Paul Keating was still in power, and the RBA was content that the outlook embodied an extended period of low inflation, subdued wage pressure, and a structural swing towards surplus in the Commonwealth budget. Australian exports were showing surprising strength. Our primary exports were legendary. Our manufacturing goods were entering international markets at competitive prices and at a pace sufficient to contribute to both domestic growth and external debt reduction. Australia's interest burden on overseas debt was falling, and funds coming into Australia increasingly would be in the form of equity investment rather than debt. The outlook for Australian productivity was strong, sufficient to reduce inflation relative to our trading partners, thus strengthening the real exchange-rate.

Final check-point: speculation aside, the Australian dollar had remained stable while Australian interest rates had fallen relative to international interest rates since 1990, a signal that underlying international and domestic investor confidence in Australia should ensure a sustained long-term growth path.

Armed with this analysis, Bernie and his team crafted their own defence strategy, aware of the evidence from the Asian experience that it could turn out to be folly to rely on good economic credentials once the hedge fund juggernaut had set itself rolling. A country's central bank could but assure itself that the cause was just, and enter the trenches.

Australia secured an alliance with the Federal Reserve in New York. At the end of each Australian working day, the RBA phoned the Fed with instructions on how far it should go in buying Australian dollars from hedge fund sellers overnight, in order to defend a predetermined level in the currency. Some nights, the transactions in New York breached the limits set in the earlier conference, and the Fed would come back to those manning the night watch at RBA headquarters at the top end of Martin Place, Sydney, asking how much further Australia was prepared to go in defence. Sometimes the answer had to lie with Bernie, rung at 2.00 or 3.00 a.m. Both the RBA and the private-sector traders realised this was a battle of strategy and discipline. So when, at any point in the hedge funds' campaign, the pressure on the currency price became sufficient to drive it down, the Australians' retreat was orderly, with troops and logistics intact.

It was gripping to watch. The hedge funds would pick some real or invented political crisis in Australia and set the blitzkrieg rolling: they would sell Australian dollars at a price below the current market price, put the word around in the London *Financial Times* and the *Wall Street Journal* that the Australian dollar was weak and vulnerable, and wait for the market price to fall below that at which they had sold so they could buy back at the lower price and deliver the currency at a profit to themselves. This process would spiral, they figured, so that it would become easier and easier to sell the Australian dollar short—to flog it down until there was no life left in it and the real parameters of the Australian economy were collapsing. But what they didn't bargain for was an Australian dollar floating so freely under private-sector market-making that it was impossible to pin it down to a point where our central bank had to pay the hedge funds ransom to go away. Such was the freedom of the Australian dollar float that the central bank was able to say: 'Do your damnedest.'

The Australian dollar fell relatively sharply against the US dollar in 1994, and again after Keating had left office in 1997 and 2000. But in none of the hedge funds' raids was there a serious prospect of the dollar breaking into a spiralling decline in the manner of the various Asian currencies. The declines in the Australian currency were always in markets overseas, and the domestic economy remained unmarked. The ultimate losers in these skirmishes were the hedge funds because, as the price of the Australian dollar recovered, they were forced to go into the market to cover their positions by buying Australian dollars at a higher price than they had contracted to sell them for. So the hedge funds lost money—an unusual experience for them.

Ironically, because the battles took place in paper-trading forays in international currency markets, the periods of a decline in value of the Australian dollar ultimately benefited our national economy. Prices for staple exports rose in Australian-dollar terms, raising the domestic buying power of those involved in export sectors across the board. There is all the difference in the world between a useful dip in a currency's value in a time of international stress, and a spiralling, spirit-breaking nosedive. Our dollar never went past the point of a useful depreciation, giving the Australian economy a timely boost in competitiveness that was useful when Australian exporters had to find alternative markets to those that that been lost in east Asia, and when products in the domestic market looked for a degree of protection.

IT IS A FURTHER IRONY that the hedge funds' assault on Australia was handled so competently that many Australians did not either realise or understand the risk that was posed to our economy during that decade. We moved on from that success to a new phase in our economic life, the boom of the 2000s; and as the money echoes of that boom begin to fade, once again, only a minority of Australians will discern how or why a new and more threatening phase of economic life is forming.

I will examine this question later. For now, it is sufficient to say that, just because a successfully floating exchange rate was able to absorb what could have been savage external shocks upon our community in the decade of the 1990s, that does not necessarily provide us with immunity in the future. The floating exchange-rate protection in the 1990s worked so well because—despite the sustained sneers of the Howard government throughout its long term of office—Paul Keating left John Howard with a domestic economy that, for a time, was pretty much a model of rectitude. Productivity was sustained at a high-enough rate to keep domestic inflation very low in the face of strongly rising demand. Prices did not rise unduly, yet profit margins kept investment rising at a pace that steadily lifted employment and tax revenues to remarkable levels.

Spurred on by the new forms of savings available to ordinary workers, the domestic savings rate continued to rise. This was a dream setting for a falling exchange rate because it meant that the internal effects of a fall in the currency's international value were benign.

This model of domestic rectitude has begun to fall away, and we now face prospects of a worsening decline. How much worse it gets depends on circumstances now largely outside our control—particularly on what China decides to do about its exchange rate. This is the situation of the Australian economy today: the golden circle has been broken. The level of total domestic savings (that is, budget surpluses, public sector and private sector combined) is well below the level of total expenditure. The current account deficit is 7 per cent, and this has exposed us to an excess of tainted offshore money—ironically, the once-pristine US dollar.

The US dollar is tainted for us because a calamity in the US homes sector has forced a continuing creep upwards in the interest costs of US bank money, and a crab-like retreat in confidence in the US financial sector overall.

The Howard government made a great show of its ability to produce good surpluses in the public sector; but in the private sector a large deficit was all the while forming, which the Howard government did nothing to control. Despite the almost ritual display of annual budget surpluses, there was no overall domestic surplus to meet the call for a larger and larger feed into private-sector credit, and so the demand for credit has been increasingly met at the margins with tainted deposits drawn from abroad.

And just as the masters of the annual budget surplus were on their way out of office, the nation found itself confronted with the evidence that this international pool of credit is indeed tainted, in the form of Australian bank cash and mortgage rate rises over and above those decreed by the Reserve Bank. The contamination is still something of a mystery to most folk, since it relates to the US property market. American bricks and mortar, it turns out, are not as safe as houses. Low interest rates and a healthy economy caused a rush of home construction and a rise in housing prices in the US in the first half of this decade; but, by 2006, home prices there began to drop as interest rates rose, supply exceeded demand, and reported foreclosures began to rise.

It was the US housing market's worst collapse in generations, and a distinctive feature of the slump was the large number of risky home loans that had been written. The phrase 'sub-prime home mortgages', now so familiar to Australians, is an American term for loans to low-income earners with deficient credit histories. Because of their inherent risk, these loans are generally written at a higher interest rate than the standard one. When the market turned, it took little time before sub-prime borrowers began defaulting on their loans, and the value of their housing assets collapsed.

So swift was the deterioration of the sub-prime capacity to service loans, and the proliferation of destroyed collateral in the hands of the mortgage lenders, that the loss of mortgage capital became a crisis. Such capital had taken the form of borrowing from a bank, so mortgage lenders in turn found themselves unable to repay their debts, and filed for bankruptcy. Almost 40 per cent of housing loans written in 2006 were at the riskier end of the spectrum, according to American reports. The significant rate of default among the mortgage lenders came as a monstrous shock to the banks. In parts of their lending portfolios they were losing money hand over fist. Their response was to drastically tighten lending conditions and raise the price of inter-bank lending; but the first precaution was too late, while the second struck at the very basis of the banking system.

Meanwhile, out in mortgage land, the contagion was spreading, spilling from the lower end of the housing market across class barriers. At the higher end of the sub-prime market, a house forced into a distressed sale was perhaps good enough to compete in the market for non-sub-prime homes; because of saturated demand, housing prices were already sagging in middle-class estates across several parts of the country. The collapse of a stable class of mortgage-brokers then combined with the increasing reluctance of the banks to lend on real estate assets, even middle-class ones. And so the almost unthinkable happened: the family asset structure in the US lost its copper-bottom base—the value of the family home.

One can only wonder where this process is going to end, but it is a fair bet that it is not going to end quickly, and so the contamination of the US dollar is not going to end quickly. Back in Australia, those of us who thought that the Howard–Costello combination was wrong when it decided not to go on with Keating's plans for increased savings through a 15 per cent contribution to superannuation can take this as new grist to their mill. The government broke economic discipline. It will turn out that the coalition's greatest crime was to allow the private-sector deficit to steadily increase under the mask of Commonwealth budget surpluses. For it is that—the Australian banks' need to increase their reliance on international bank loans—which has suddenly, and unforeseeably, exposed us to the financial meltdown in the American heartland. Our banks and other financial institutions are now not only exposed to the rising cost of US inter-bank loans, but indirectly to their bad debts.

Had the sub-prime mortgage crisis formed part of the background to the hedge fund attacks of the 1990s, the significant downward pressure on the Australian exchange rate would have been far more harmful than it was. Our economy would have been much more fragile in a setting where our bankers had to face rising interest rates overseas that were driven by a malignant force beyond the control of our Reserve Bank. In that situation, the combination of a rapidly falling Australian currency and unpredictable rises in the cost of overseas borrowing would have created fatal business conditions for Australian financial establishments.

At the start of 2008, the value of the Australian dollar was high, but the outlook for the global economy was uncertain. President Bush, with the nervous support of an otherwise truculent Congress, introduced a series of tax cuts and industry-boosting measures that, he assured the world, in his agonisingly unbelievable way, would 'revitalise' the 'large and dynamic' US economy. The measures were real and quite substantial yet Wall Street paid them little notice. For good reason. It sensed, accurately, that George Bush's rhetoric was dodging the main issue. And that issue, of course, is the unknown and unknowable potential for the rot in the US housing market to spread and to keep on spreading, regardless of how much money is thrown into stimulating the American economy.

This same note of unreality permeates the comments of more sober-sided people such as the heads of central banks. Their assurances are not very convincing because, just like the rest of us, they seem not to have grasped the full potential for disaster which lies in the unprecedented mix of financial malfunction, social disintegration, and human despair and bitterness that lies at the heart of sub-prime mortgage crisis.

Australia's Reserve Bank governor, Glenn Stevens, a contemporary model of po-faced officialdom, invokes bureaucratic newspeak when he tells us the main danger to Australia and the world is not that of a spill-over of slow demand from the US (that is, the thing that George Bush is diligently fixing), but rather a 'commonality' of financial crises. By this, he means there is a danger that the collapse of financial arrangements for homes and other assets in financially stressed areas of the United States may spread internationally.

This fear of a 'commonality' is well founded; we have already seen how the virus can jump continents. Because problem sub-prime mortgages had been parcelled into high-yielding packages and 'securitised'—made into units that can be traded as investment paper throughout the sophisticated financial world—the US disease has appeared in Europe and Asia. British advisors who had previously pronounced that the sub-prime mortgage crisis was a local American phenomenon had to revise their statements when packages that contained within them slices of US sub-prime mortgages turned up in the portfolios of British banks. Because of losses on securitised US sub-prime mortgage packages, the Northern Rock bank, a former building society based in Newcastle upon Tyne, was forced to seek emergency protection from the Bank of England. Northern Rock and others like it sharply tightened the terms and extent of their mortgage lending; mortgage-brokers started to go under. The American symptoms were soon on display in Britain. How far the problem will extend in Britain remained unclear at the time of writing.

And in Australia? The threat of sub-prime 'commonality'

establishing itself here is less than in the US or Britain, because Australian society is more fungible than American or British. Fungible means 'interchangeable, mixable'; it is a word not often used outside law or finance, but I find it useful here to analyse social mobility. The US, in particular, is less fungible than Australia because it still has a relatively rigidly confined African–American under-class. It was among poor blacks, largely, that the sub-prime crisis started. Because banking conditions and credit in the US became easier than they had ever been before, some mortgage-brokers began offering deals on housing in repressed African-American and poor white communities that these folk had never been offered before. In too many cases, the deals collapsed.

Because of the social segmentation involved, the mortgage crises in this stratum were left to fester to the point of becoming gangrenous. Left this way, the infection worsened in a confined portion of the American corpus until, when it did finally break out, it did so virulently. Real estate operators suddenly found they were trying to sell houses on one side of town as brightly shining asset-growth bases, when you could walk 50 yards across the tracks and get one for nothing. So, from this state, the infection spread. Australia certainly has class pockets, both ethnic and economic, but nothing like this. Relatively speaking, we are too 'interchangeable, mixable' for such an infection to become concentrated to bursting point. The threat here is that the international financial malaise will worsen, hurting us by association through US dollar borrowings.

We start from a relatively comfortable position in which the $A/$US exchange rate is high, due largely to soaring international terms of trade in favour of Australia. The Australian dollar exchange rate is in part a function of our terms of trade, and our terms of trade are in part a function of the prices of internationally traded commodities. Prices for many of the goods we export—iron ore, beef, wheat, wool, oil, natural gas, and base metals—have surged in recent years, particularly in relation to the prices of imports. This relationship determines our terms of trade and thus influences our exchange rate. While the terms of trade remain so strong, our exchange rate remains strong, and it would take a fair amount of shocks from the sub-prime crisis to send it down, particularly to levels that would force punitive domestic adjustments.

But the tocsin bell rings in the need for Australian banks to lift their cash rates higher than those dictated by the policy-led rises of the Reserve Bank. Thus far out of earshot is China, in particular the pressure on that country to adjust its managed-exchange-rate policy to cope better with domestic pressures.

One can see persistent question marks flashing for Australia in both the United States and Japan, and I will consider these later. But China is perhaps the ace in the hole that is going to determine which way the balance goes for Australia. Our powerful trading partner is the key to Australian commodity prices. A fair part of the rise in the Australian dollar in recent years has been due to the fact that the Chinese leadership has deliberately kept the Chinese currency, the yuan, undervalued, in order to channel resources away from the consumer economy and towards manufacturing and infrastructure investment, and thus the importing of raw materials. Our medium-term future—financial and economic—depends on how long this stance holds in the face of inadequate Chinese domestic responses to health, transport, and general household problems.

More than any other country, Australia has benefited from

the Chinese currency-management policy, which is certainly not a benefit to the ordinary Chinese householder. In effect, the strengthening of both the Australian currency and real incomes have been dependent upon Chinese policy, and Australian securities markets have benefited through Chinese reinvestment of the huge reserves that build up with an undervalued currency. There is now, though, greater and greater pressure inside China to switch its currency-management approach from an undervaluation of the yuan to a 'normalised' valuation, so that the Chinese economy can begin to switch from satisfying export industries to satisfying a domestic demand for a more rewarding home market. A more inward-looking Chinese dictatorship would mean a more affluent Chinese household population—with less focus on heavy industry, and more focus on consumer goods and services for local markets.

A 'normalised' valuation would mean a sudden, official up-valuation of the Chinese currency. And any deliberate appreciation of the yuan would mean lower commodity prices for Australia. It is the consideration of this point that is causing European forecasters to come up with $A projections that would see the Australian dollar plunging against the US dollar from its level of around 94 US cents in April 2008 to perhaps 66 cents in 2010. If this scenario proves anything like accurate, our dangerously growing dependence on overseas borrowing could leave our economy more and more exposed.

We are not in the trim condition that we were in the 1990s, when major fluctuations of the Australian dollar could run their course externally, exciting currency markets in New York and London without leading to an adverse effect on the domestic economy. Pressure on domestic resources is already too tight, and demand for domestic credit is spilling over into ever-unpredictable international financial markets. We are about to learn the hard way how far we have strayed from the path of fiscal rectitude into the economic wilderness since Paul Keating reluctantly handed in his prime ministerial commission.

Part II
Into the Wilderness

Chapter 8

Star-crossed Mates

'On me the tempest falls. It does not make me tremble. O holy Mother Earth, O air and sun, behold me. I am wronged.' –*Prometheus Bound*, Aeschylus

BERNIE FRASER WAS THE EPITOME OF A SUCCESSFUL, LABOR-oriented public servant. His father had been an itinerant bush worker who had established a home at Junee in southern New South Wales. It was there that Bernie went diligently to state school and played rugby league, the workingman's game. He played league with sufficient enthusiasm to have his nose seriously broken. He matriculated from Junee High School to study economics at the University of New England, and by dint of hard work and substantial capacity rose steadily through the ranks of the Commonwealth public service, until he stood among those senior men of the Treasury who had graduated from Oxford, Cambridge, the Massachusetts Institute of Technology, the Wharton School of the University of Pennsylvania, and similar places.

Bernie replaced John Stone as secretary of the Treasury in 1984. Paul Keating felt particularly warm and comfortable about this: for the first time, a Labor-oriented coterie of mates led by Bernie at Treasury surrounded the Labor treasurer. Keating was at the head of the round table. He was Prince Hal in place of King Arthur.

Perhaps in compensation for what he was about to do in other areas of policy, Keating came to power with certain left-leaning predilections against what he then saw as the establishment: he wanted to get rid of the monarchy's constitutional role, he wanted to change the flag, he wanted to break the central bank's practice of drawing its governors from within its own apolitical ranks. When the time next came for change at the top of the bank, he wanted a Labor protégé from his round table at the head of the central bank.

As it turned out, there were fatal contradictions in what he wanted. He wanted a Reserve Bank independent of government for the first time; independently endowed to set policy as it thought fit, whether the government liked it or not. Instead of being just a bond-selling agency for the Treasury, the Reserve Bank would be the power centre for monetary policy: it would have the same status in Australia that the US Federal Reserve has in America.

This was most commendable of Keating; but he also wanted to assume a Napoleonic capacity himself—in the sense of taking quick, strategic action—in the area of monetary policy. Certainly, he would more likely be able to do this with a mate from his round table at the top of the bank. But there were factors of human nature involved here that made his actions concerning Bernie—concerning anyone in the position in which he had placed Bernie—a perilous course.

They turned out to be star-crossed mates, Bernie and Paul, and from this a tragedy unfolded. However, the faults lay not in the stars but in themselves. Keating should have seen the contradiction between wanting to act as Napoleon at Austerlitz—wanting to instruct his marshals to feint left and right on monetary policy and then to drive down the centre—and, at the same time, respecting the independence he had pronounced for the Reserve Bank. Fraser should have realised that he was accepting the job of presiding over interest rates from a treasurer who knew enough about interest rates to find it almost impossible to keep his hands away when he judged that monetary policy needed to change.

It is remarkable, though, given these circumstances, how far Paul Keating managed to go towards eschewing policy interference in interest rates—even to the ultimate point of losing office over the Reserve Bank's interest-rate action. In 1988, Bob Johnston, Fraser's predecessor as Australian central bank governor, had returned from an international central bankers' meeting at Basle convinced that we were going back to 1929 conditions. He began listing the names of Australian punters who would go under to the tune of tens of billions of dollars—Murdoch, Bond, Holmes à Court—taking Australia into another Great Depression with them. So Keating kept his hands off monetary policy, even though his instincts for the Austerlitz game told him that the correct tactics here were to sacrifice his right flank—speculative builders and, if necessary, a Murdoch or a Bond—by raising interest rates sharply in 1988 in order to hack into mounting business credit.

While Bob Johnston mulled on the sombre tones of Basle, business credit in Australia continued to surge, eventually running above 30 per cent per annum in growth. To prevent a slump into recession in 1990, it was necessary that the credit-surge peak well short of this. By the time Johnston was ready to engineer a substantial interest rate rise through 1989, a speculative building boom had surged to its own bursting peak and was on its way sharply down.

'I wanted commercial interest rates to go high enough here to slow the building boom well short of the speculative peak it reached. In my mind, that was the way to save the wages accord without inducing a 1929 here. Otherwise, I knew a blowout was on its way,' Keating told me later. 'Astute government required that rates be got up quickly enough to flatten the boom that was concentrated in housing, in property. Then when you had done that, you got interest rates down quickly—quickly enough to flatten the downswing.'

When Bob Johnston left the RBA in 1989, the economy was decelerating rapidly into recession. It was not a good time for a proud bushman's son to take over. Bernie Fraser faced a board on which the only representative of the working class was another of Paul Keating's mates, Bill Kelty. The rest were mainly businessmen. Keating had broken the practice of appointing apolitical bank insiders to the governorship. The phrase of the day from the Liberal opposition was that Keating had the Reserve Bank in his pocket: this was completely wrong, as it would later turn out. Given the statistics, Keating didn't have to have Bernie Fraser in his pocket to expect him to smartly cut interest rates. As employment and production began to fall, the Australian commercial banks' indicator rate was close to 20 per cent, and the housing loan rate was at 17 per cent.

The dilemma Fraser faced was obvious. The greater part of the business view on his board was that rates had to come down. But there was one senior businessman vehemently against this: in his view, after the property boom, Australia had to take a squeeze. Because keeping rates up was a matter of not acting, Bernie opted for signalling a desire for unanimity on the board by not acting. He declined to agree with Keating's urgent remonstrations for a rate cut.

'I said to Bernie, "We've got to be quick and flexible. This is the time to go into reverse." But there was on the bank board at that time a standout against this. I've got the picture of him still fixed in my mind: he wore black suits and looked like a bad priest. I said to Bernie, "Take no notice of him, he has become an old fool."

'But Bernie wanted to keep his board in unison. He said he had to put a high priority on holding the board as one. And I wanted to strengthen Bernie's faith in himself as an independent central banker, like the head of the US Federal Reserve. So we did nothing. He wouldn't go against this black fool, and the price of not going against him was that the monetary goose got well and truly overcooked.'

By the time that business-indicator interest rates began to fall from their peak of 20 per cent in 1990, capacity-utilisation rates in industry were already falling, retail trade growth was at zero level, building approvals had dropped sharply, private-sector job vacancies were falling, and business confidence was on the wane. The interest-rate weapon was being used to attack an already-weakening economy, which was far from a demonstration of impressive economic generalship. As Keating later lamented, 'Bernie's desire to build unison in the bank meant that those rates stayed up much longer than they should have.' The result was that, in 1990–91, Australia went into recession. Keating dubbed it the 'recession we had to have'. It was deeper than Keating would have preferred, but they could live with that, he told Kelty.

Bill Kelty was aware that something was quite awry in

the mates' formula here. He knew as well as Keating that, to smooth the economy, interest rates should have been falling by mid-1989 at the latest, and he told his friend so. Keating found himself in the galling position of having to defend both himself and Bernie to Bill. The passage of events demonstrated that Keating's choice of Fraser was a mixed bag indeed. Certainly, in picking a man of such strength of mind as Bernie Fraser, Paul Keating had the right man to lead the bank independently. But what of the golden circle? Bill Kelty asked. You will see, Paul said to Bill; Bernie would also have enough sense, and by now enough experience, to keep monetary policy on a course towards a closing path for the golden circle. But Kelty was not impressed, 'You'd better watch him,' he said. 'He's a stubborn bastard.' This exchange between Keating and Kelty on the relative strengths of Fraser was ongoing, and the worst of it was yet to come.

Fifteen years later, Ian Macfarlane, the man who replaced Bernie Fraser as governor in 1996, would say that he felt able to praise his institution highly (and by inference, presumably, Paul Keating) for the way it had so strategically deflated the economy in 1990. This sharp deflation produced one of the steepest dives in Australian inflationary expectations in our history—from forward expectations of an inflation rate of 10 per cent per annum in 1990, to 3 per cent by 1992. But what most observers ignored during this period was that the inflation rate never got anywhere near the level expected, due largely to the remarkable resilience of the wage accord between the unions and the government earlier in the 1980s, and this in part was due to the fact that the unions had agreed to have part of their wage bargain in the form of contributions to the pension funds that Bill Kelty had sold them, in lieu of cash in hand. Real unit-labour costs had dropped from an annual growth of 6 per cent under the Fraser government to near zero. And through the early years of the 1990s Australian market productivity had surged.

Certainly, the downward jolt of 1990 ensured that the Australian consumer-price inflation rate ran into the new decade at a rate of 2 per cent per annum, which was lower than the inflation index for the traditional low-inflation countries of the OECD, namely Austria, Germany, Japan, Netherlands, and Switzerland.

Keating must have viewed this high praise from Ian Macfarlane for the RBA under Bernie Fraser with some wry satisfaction. At the very least, it gave the lie to the Howard–Costello team's oft-repeated assertion that they were the ones who began Australia's long run as a low-inflation, high-productivity economy.

But only Paul and Bernie and Bill could have known that, had Bernie made some meaningful concession to Paul's urgings on the timing of interest-rate changes, they could have achieved the same low inflation with an even higher rate of productivity. For Keating, the most disappointing aspect of this period was the demonstration that Fraser was not going to be Marshal Ney to his Napoleon.

THE TRAGEDY OF BERNIE AND PAUL as star-crossed mates was far from over. Two-and-a-half years after Paul Keating had returned from exile and become prime minister, there was an extraordinary instance of Reserve Bank-induced monetary deflation that makes the charge that Paul Keating had Bernie Fraser in his pocket one of cruel absurdity. Consider the facts over a crucial run of years.

Though production recovered from its low point in 1991, it did not do so quickly enough to lead business decision-makers to put in new capacity, and this must be the ultimate test of the severity of a recession. Employment and household spending can slump sufficiently to meet the statistical definition of a recession (two consecutive quarters of falling national product). But this does not always set back the business psyche to the point where decision-makers cancel plans to add to new capacity and build stocks from existing capacity. There are recessions and recessions, although the most popularly watched markers may be the same.

During the slow recovery from the 1990–91 recession, seasoned decision-makers noted that, while production was well into positive-growth territory again by the end of 1992, business credit-growth was still falling in 1993, and business spending on new capacity and new stocks in preparation for an upturn was slight. New dwelling commencements, which had reached a peak of a 30 per cent annual increase in the previous upswing, were still at negative levels after the recession had officially ended. By early 1994, a majority of companies were still expressing an adverse view of the outlook.

A drought in eastern Australia had sent the price of fruit and vegetables sharply up by early 1994. The consumer-price inflation rate, which had been running at 2 per cent, bumped temporarily to 4 per cent. The price rise was an aberration in an economy so flat that the prime minister did not think it worth raising the question of demand-pull inflation with his advisors. There wasn't any: there were unavoidable price bumps on the supply side, and to react to them with anti-inflationary demand-control measures would be unwarranted, indeed dangerous.

Much to Paul Keating's amazement, the Reserve Bank began using its new independence to raise official rates in mid-1994, and to go on raising them over the course of six months until the overall increase was 2.75 percentage points: that is, a rise from 4.75 per cent to 7.5 per cent, a structural rise of almost 60 per cent. Some indication of the enormity of this action is gained by contemplating the hand-wringing and outpourings of angst that go on today over a rise of 0.25 percentage points in cash rates.

Contributing to technical inflation readings through the period were increases in taxes on cigarettes and tobacco, petrol, and motor vehicles. The dominant factor in Australian price increases in these six months, however, was the increase in mortgage payments due to the increase in Reserve Bank-induced cash rates: here was the inflation snake feeding on itself on the supply side. Any competent high school student of economics could have told the Reserve Bank that this was not a setting in which to raise interest rates as an anti-inflationary measure, especially not by 2.75 percentage points. The production economy was flat, the climate in business was deteriorating, and the home investment movement had reversed itself from the late 1980s boom.

Just what Bernie Fraser and his Reserve Bank colleagues thought they were doing in this period, they have never bothered to explain. Ian Macfarlane told a business economists' gathering in Sydney: 'The episode in Australia which returned us to a low-inflation, stable growth economy was regarded as a policy error, whereas in America it is regarded as a policy triumph for us.'

This episode might be regarded as a policy triumph in some Swiftian land where the ascendant system of government is government by central banks, whatever that might be called. But, in Australia, government is the epitome of the political. Success in government is achieved by treading a fine line between left and right. Victory is achieved by one's cleverness in manipulating the press to put a scare up the people, principally either by creating a danger from the north or creating the danger of sharp interest-rate rises under one's opponents. To represent as a policy triumph a period of increasing interest rates far more than is necessary provides a good insight into the mindset of the Reserve Bank at that time. Either deliberately or unwittingly, they had no conception of (or regard for) the political implications of what they were doing.

You might say that this was a good thing, and three cheers for Ian Macfarlane and Bernie Fraser. But the costs of what they did are great and much more difficult to trace than deflationary action itself and the period of 'low inflation, stable growth'. The profound political costs include the following: John Howard's dangerous distortion of political history in which he represented Keating's final years as a policy mess giving way to his own decade and more of economic sunshine. At Keating's expense, Fraser and his Reserve Bank cleared the field for a marvellous period of extended non-inflationary growth under Howard, and Howard and Costello have nurtured the myth that it was all their doing.

Blind Freddie could have run a champion economy after the Reserve Bank's preparation of a deflated ground in the early to middle 1990s. But more important to me is the fact that the Reserve Bank's actions unconsciously cleared the way for Howard and Costello's destruction of the Keating timetable towards a workers' pension of 15 per cent by year 2000, and of all the invaluable turbo-charging of the capital market and expansion of the new export industry based on financial services that would have been attendant on that.

BY GETTING RID OF KEATING EARLY, the Reserve Bank joined Howard and Costello in crudely curtailing the most fruitful period of financial reform this country has ever experienced. We must believe that the bank knew not what it did; but to stay for a moment within the environs of that phrase, the bank deserves as much contumely as Pontius Pilate did in the context of the original utterance.

This book is more than an attempt at righting economic history in a very important, complex, and insufficiently understood period of our growth. It is also, to some extent, about men's souls and the way in which eternal irony can shape what happens to people in public life who have enough imagination and foresight to try to make great changes. Paul Keating felt sure he had a soul mate in Bernie Fraser. Without compromising the independence that, as head of the central bank, Keating insisted Fraser must have, Paul felt sure that Bernie would nonetheless be very careful not to destroy his patron. But that is precisely what Fraser and his Reserve Bank high command inadvertently accomplished.

As the bank pushed the policy cash rate to complete a full rise of 2.75 percentage points through the second six months of 1994, Paul Keating looked out the window and saw that, along with the rapid march upwards in interest rates, dwelling commencements had already fallen to a negative rate of growth, business sentiment had fallen into negative balance, credit was at a zero rate of growth, construction and manufacturing output had fallen to a zero growth rate, employment had fallen to a zero growth rate, and so had real unit-labour costs. What were they doing, these newly independent central bankers? His acute political sense told him that he was finished. He was to be executed for a crime he did not commit.

As the election in the first half of 1996 drew closer, and the economy failed to revive, the omens of a terrible loss fell upon Keating. As the leader of an egalitarian party, Keating had kept hidden an image he had of himself as a man of destiny. But deep down he knew himself to be a rare bird, as rare birds do. In every generation, a person arises with a capacity well above the ordinary in foresight and in the ability to lead their community to greater things. Keating had come to see this as a responsibility placed upon him. The defeat coming towards him now was almost unimaginable, but as plain as the nose on his face.

It is part of the art of politics to be able to accept defeat as a setback and to move on. Part of Keating told him that he was more than enough of a professional to accept this. Another part told him that defeat at this time would result in his personal and political annihilation. The process has been captured forever in Shakespeare's lines on the fall of Cardinal Wolsey in *Henry VIII*:

> This is the state of man: today he puts forth
> The tender leaves of hopes, tomorrow blossoms,
> And bears his blushing honours thick upon him;
> The third day comes a frost, a killing frost,
> And when he thinks, good easy man, full surely
> His greatness is a-ripening, nips his root
> And then he falls as I do.

In Keating's case, the killing frost came early, and was not of his own making. People both for and against Keating have said that he brought the 1996 defeat upon himself. He was going to lose the 1996 election for any number of reasons. In particular, he was too arrogant; he was not a team player; he treated his ministers with derision; and by the end of his term, he was no longer working hard enough. John Button, one of his economic ministers, said he did not speak to the people: 'He spoke to the elites and not the masses who felt he was not interested in them.' Gerard Henderson put it this way: 'He was a smartarse and Australians don't like a smartarses.'

If Keating's political demise was due to these things, he would not be worth bothering about. However, in a community obsessed with interest rates and home prices, it seems quite incredible that so very few have grasped the fact that, less than 18 months before an election, a rise of 60 per cent in the interest-rate base of an economy is of itself enough to kill even the most golden incumbency. No amount of morning walks, teetotalism, or tolerance of nongs will save you from the effect of this.

The 1994 central bank interest-rate policy makes Keating, for all his faults, a Promethean figure. In Greek mythology, the god Prometheus was a real operator. He clashed with the father of the gods, Zeus, because the two had different estimates of the worth of mankind. Zeus saw no value in mortals, so he intended man to live as a primitive until he died off; he had concluded that knowledge and divine gifts would be wasted on the beggars. Prometheus saw the species differently: he equipped them with abilities in brick-working, woodworking, agriculture, numbers, letters, transportation, herbal medicine, art, and other things.

To complete the package, he stole fire from heaven to allow

his mortals to develop from what he had given them, and this unleashed a flood of inventiveness and productivity on the part of man. Zeus was furious, not so much at the theft, but rather because he had been proven wrong. He had Hephaestus shackle Prometheus to a crag high in the Caucasean Mountains. Then Zeus sent an eagle to torment Prometheus forever; each day the eagle would tear into the flesh around Prometheus's liver. The flesh would heal overnight, and next day the eagle would start again.

Keating delivered the Australian people a considerable package of gifts. He saw what might happen if you removed the insular pomposity of Australian banking. He freed the dollar to make it a currency of world standing—the top dollar in Asia. He built on John Hewson's work to free the bond market to make it a national force as well articulated as it is in New York. He reformed business tax in favour of yield and, having done so, in combination with Bill Kelty, he created a workers' superannuation system in such a way that it could take over imputed earnings and market yields, and turn the Australian capital market into one of the strongest in the world. He began balancing our external current-account deficit with domestic savings, sufficiently to prevent Australia from being part of the terrible destruction that overtook our northern neighbours late in the twentieth century. But before he had finished his work, the metaphorical eagle was onto him.

In subsequent years he sat in his office off Macleay Street, Sydney, chained to a Promethean rock—a prisoner of public opinion, if you prefer—and, daily, his enemies pecked at his vitals.

I WENT TO SEE PAUL KEATING in his rooms in Sydney soon after his government's defeat in March 1996. I had not, at this time, satisfied myself completely about the process of the untimely elevation of official interest rates and its consequences that had put him out of office. But I thought I had it right, and I wanted to get his reaction. I asked him what he thought that, more than anything else, had caused his defeat.

'Oh, I think it was no one thing in particular,' he said. 'Bob Hawke and I had done a lot to secure the economy, and I think people just thought they were out of the woods—things would be looking up, but they probably could move a bit faster. So it was time for a change.'

I was, and I remain, politically agnostic. But this pathetic plaint I could not stand. It angered me to hear Keating ready to cast himself away with uncharacteristic, bland politeness.

'For Christ's sake, Paul, that's not right,' I said. 'Look through the graphs in the Reserve Bank's own quarterly report, and you can see that extraordinary rates lift in 1994. You must stop making allowances for mates, and admit it was a misguided disaster, amounting finally to a gift to John Howard. You owe it to Bill Kelty, who stuck with you through all this with the wages accord, not to let this go with just a whimper.'

I had in my briefcase a copy of the eighth round of the wages accord process. In part, it noted that the accord was based on and consistent with an underlying rate of 2 to 3 per cent of inflation over the cycle. This was essential if interest rates were to remain at levels 'conducive to economic and employment growth', it said. The document noted that underlying inflation had remained at this 2 to 3 per cent level. Bernie Fraser and the board of the bank must have known of this attitude of the union leadership in mid-1994—because Bill Kelty was on the board. Indeed, Kelty was the only member of the board to vote against the interest-rate hikes. In the light of this, I said, it had been irresponsible for the bank to lift official rates in the way that they did.

I had provoked Paul Keating out of his slump: 'Bill Kelty said at the board, you know, what do you want to do this for? The underlying inflation rate is not changing. What we have got to worry about here is wages, and the accord is holding wages. Wages are running at 4.5 per cent, conducive with an underlying inflation rate of 2 per cent. So why are you tilting at windmills?'

Keating continued: 'But Bernie said to Bill, no, no. We've got the inflation rate down, and we are damn-well going to keep it down. In effect, he was saying that the moment we see any sort of green shoot of inflation, we are going to burn it. The trouble is, he burned everything around it, including the government.'

'Including you,' I said.

'Including me, yes. Bill said on the board that the unions were pledged—and would remain pledged in the coming eighth round of the accord—to run wages growth at no more than 5 per cent alongside a 2.5 per cent productivity growth, which was consistent with an underlying 2.5 per cent prices growth. This was the greatest commonsense we have had from the unions in a lifetime. And the structure for that commonsense is now departing from the scene.'

Paul Keating went on to rifle through files on his desk and produced some Treasury briefing sheets, one of which he triumphantly produced to show effective tariffs rates from 1968 through to 1996. They showed the effective Australian tariff on footwear, clothing, textiles, and leather reaching an extraordinary peak above 150 per cent in 1983 and then swiftly falling to 20 per cent by 1996. Motor vehicles and parts followed the same trajectory of decline at a lower level. The total manufacturing tariff followed a less dramatic trajectory downward. It was like a man going through pictures of old girlfriends. He shuffled them and put them back in a file.

'One thing I suppose I must be grateful for is that Howard has undertaken to keep the build-up in workers' superannuation going towards a higher percentage of the wage,' he said. 'And the papers have pinned him on this.' He turned towards another file of newspaper clippings. 'This is in the *Australian* a month before the election from Don Greenlees: "Opposition leader Howard guaranteed that a Coalition government would pay the full round of the $3.5 billion in tax cuts to go into the superannuation funds."'

Then he said, 'The *Age* says much the same thing: "Mr Howard yesterday raised the prospect of taxpayers getting the full benefit of Mr Keating's further round of co-payments into the superannuation funds."

'We must be grateful for this because Australia's ability to go on selling these new financial products to the rest of the world—the new industry that has started up in the wake of opening our financial markets—is going to depend more and more on the industry super funds continuing to progress towards my target of 15 per cent.

'More than anything else, now I desire that this superannuation program continue building because the underlying dynamics are so important to Australia—in so many ways, not just for adequate incomes for people over 60. Since Kelty and I started this workers' pension policy, it has been a practical joy to me to grasp what can follow from it: the turbo-charging of the capital markets so that we can go into all this exporting of financial product; the weighing of the external account deficit against savings.'

What Keating could not know then was that Howard would not keep his promise. He would stop the increase in the rate of compulsory super contributions in its tracks.

Chapter 9

A Prime Minister's Lament

'I think it will be a clash between the political will and the administrative won't.' –*Yes Prime Minister*

THE EXTRAORDINARY MATTER OF THE RESERVE BANK'S punishing interest-rate policy in the twilight of Paul Keating's prime ministership drew me back again before he left his official Sydney office in 1996. I asked him: 'Did you ever speak to Bernie Fraser about what was going to come from that scorched-earth monetary policy he launched into in 1994?'

'Of course I did,' he answered. 'I poked in front of him the renewed union commitment to keep an inflation rate between 2 and 3 per cent. I said to him, "It can't be wages driving your interest policy, Bernie, so just what is it? He said to me, "I'm worried about a return to an inflationary psychology. We have to let people know that we are not going to let inflation off the ground again."

'And this because of a fruit and vegetables spike? "Bernie," I said, "this is going to be a very big cost to activity and confidence. It will be a cost to the government; it will be a killing cost to me."

'But his attitude made it clear that the only way I could have been able to stop what was happening was to direct the bank. And after all I had put into it, that I couldn't do. When a government uses the Reserve Bank Act and tables in the House of Representatives an instruction to alter monetary policy, then the bank's standing as an independent vehicle is finished.

'Despite what I sensed then, that his policy change was going to do me in, I wasn't prepared to do that: I'd spent a decade trying to build the bank, to take it from the bond-selling agent it was to the stand-alone institution of quality it is today. I couldn't pull the carpet straight from under them.'

'So you let them pull the carpet straight from under you,' I said.

'I suppose I did, yes.'

'If you look at the business surveys for the time,' I continued. 'Look at the National Bank survey, the ACCI Westpac survey. And you can say that not only did the scene not need the 275 basis points interest lift it got, it didn't need any lift whatsoever.'

'You're right; it required none. And, what was worse, the Reserve Bank didn't pull the rates off once it saw the sag that was so clearly occurring. What it will do now is keep the rates running as they are for a time into the Howard ascendancy and then drop them. And, to the ordinary bloke, this is going to be Howard's first big achievement—getting interest rates down sharply. I put this point to Bernie. And he said that to cut rates so close to an election would be seen as political. Can you believe that? Political. By saying that to me they implied that they should have been cut. They'll be political, all right, by giving Howard a starting advantage that he isn't entitled to.'

'Paul, this is pathetic.' I said. 'Bernie was your protégé. He would never have gone from the Treasury to governorship of the Reserve Bank without you. That's not how they appoint Reserve Bank governors. But by putting those rates up like he did, he let you swing.'

'OK. For what it's worth now, let me say it: the Reserve Bank's 1994 monetary policy decisions were a very bad policy misjudgement. Inflation was not at risk. The ACTU had actually adopted the Reserve Bank's favoured policy on wages; therefore this didn't have to happen. A fair comment is that the Reserve Bank has been very hard on my government, which had already broken the back of inflation, which had carried all of the political costs of the 1989 levels of interest rates and the recession which followed, and which had paid for the wages accord. Having acted with the responsibility that we did, it was a very tough thing for the Reserve Bank to do what it did in 1994.'

I could not help but be aware that there was a sadness in Paul Keating making this statement, without the expletives and the scouring vernacular that is characteristic of him on such occasions. His clerkish delivery suggested he was holding back.

He went on: 'There is this view in the bureaucracy that political government is there to cop it: never give the suckers an even break or, if you can manage it, never give the cabinet an even break. If it is necessary for what is deemed to be good government, political government is there to be worn out. That is what happened to me. The Keating government was worn out by jumping through policy hoops which the Reserve Bank put in place.

'I agree with you: people would have expected Bernie Fraser, appointed by me, to have taken my view. John Hewson used to say in an earlier epoch that Bernie Fraser operated monetary policy to suit me, and so, he said, had his predecessor at the bank, Bob Johnston. Bob Johnston went out of his way to refute this publicly. Bernie Fraser hasn't been in a position to do that. But he didn't have to: anyone with two ounces of sense could see that Bernie Fraser wasn't operating monetary policy to suit me.

'I'm told that Bernie saw me as the man in the asbestos suit, that I could take any amount of fire and still come out on top, that I would jump through any hoop that was put in front of me that the bureaucracy thought I needed to jump. Because I had been prepared to go along with the interest-rate structure of 1989–90, I would take 2.75 percentage points in 1994 in my stride. But I knew I couldn't carry any monkey on my back this time and beat three different opposition leaders in four years—Hewson in 1993, Downer in 1994, and now Howard in 1996.

'You see, before Bob Hawke and I came along, government in Australia moved this way: Sir Frederic Wheeler, Sir Arthur Tange, and the like would get over in the Commonwealth Club in Canberra of a Friday night and work out how to move things along incrementally. All of a sudden, along comes a government that makes completely radical changes. And it doesn't do it for a year or two years; it does it for a decade. The bureaucracy watches this with fascination, and it notes that this radical government keeps on winning.

'The bureaucracy saw us continuing to do amazing things, whether it be in tariffs, electricity, telecommunications, ports, wages, the currency, financial policy. And the bureaucracy gets to feel that the way for it to operate is to just keep loading things on the donkey's back, without thinking that at some point it's going to overload the donkey; that political government will reach the point where it cannot continue to both fight off its enemies and carry the load. That's fundamentally what happened to us.

'The public service had no ill will towards us. But they didn't realise that they had to help a great reforming government stay alive. I suppose it was inevitable that they got a bit selfish about the policy demands they were making; they have assumed that I would just continue to run with whatever stones I was carrying on my back. There is no malice in it, just miscalculation.

'The Reserve Bank wanted to make a crushing blow against inflation, and thought that I would be able to run it on through the election. But this was one carry too far. I have a very fatalistic view about these things; leaders who are prepared to punt their political futures don't come very often and, when they do, the system eventually pushes this punt too far.

'There is a point, too, where you wear the public out. One is a bit like a candle: for some time you light up the room but finally the candle burns down. Your political stocks recede. You have to foresee that and to know that you are not going to be around indefinitely. Knowing that, you must get what you need to do done as quickly as you can. You must not be a mouse.

'I moved with constant awareness of this. I knew I had to move while I had such a wonderful set of cards in my hands. I had a set of trade union allies prepared to curtail their people and to keep wages down in the face of pressure. I had both unions and industry prepared to cooperate with one another in a surge of productivity. I had a really top-rate Treasury and a Reserve Bank committed against inflation. While we had that combination we could keep running. But we stumbled and fell on a difference of judgement with the Reserve Bank.

'The great cost of 1996 will not be that my prime

ministership ended, but that the reform program has finished just short of the line, just crucially short of the line. I think it comes down to misjudgement with the best of wills. The bureaucracy was so committed to me that they thought I was Man Mountain Dean; I could get anything done. Mostly, it has worked. And the crowning final run will be after I am gone and the superannuation moves quickly to the 15 per cent.

'What we've learned here is that when you are creating an institution anew like the Reserve Bank, the scope for conflict of purposes is always there. What do you do: do you let smaller points of conflict go and only challenge on the major points? Do you resist challenge altogether, even though the Reserve Bank Act allows for political government to challenge the bank? I decided I couldn't challenge, even though the political stake was so very big.'

JUST HOW BIG the political stake and personal stakes were for Keating was revealed six months after the 1996 election, when the Coalition dismantled the final part of the Keating push towards a national employees' superannuation scheme founded on 15 per cent of workers' wages.

The new treasurer, Peter Costello, killed off the progression planned by Keating, so that the contribution rate was capped at 9 per cent. It became an illustration of something that often happens in politics and public life: an arbitrary figure can take on a life of its own and run on as received wisdom without rhyme or reason. The 9 per cent superannuation figure, which is now known to every businessman and trade union official in the country, has no basis in economic or social logic. It just happened to be the ratio of superannuation payments to wages applying at the time that Keating's last budget ran out.

On the other hand, the target of 15 per cent by 2000 towards which Keating had aimed his 1995–96 budget does have a substantial point in logic. It was set following objective advice to Keating that this was the level at which a middle-income earner could know that he or she was prepared for a comfortable old age. It also had the virtue of equating national savings to national spending at a level that would limit foreign borrowings and contain our external debt to levels that could forever be benign.

After the defeat of the Keating government, and the denial of the inferences previously given by John Howard during the election campaign that his government would go on with the 'co-payments' progress to a higher degree of government-sponsored employee superannuation payments, I began to do some research. How was it that the progression, first to 12 per cent and then to the ultimate 15 per cent, had so completely disappeared off the official radar?

I worked at the top of Treasury on an off-the-record basis, and discovered that the 15 per cent calculation had originated from within Treasury itself. Concerned at the prospective burden of a rapidly ageing population, Treasury staff had been working on this since the late 1980s. Paul Keating as treasurer and prime minister had picked up on their work, and his imagination had fixed upon it as he saw how the 15 per cent figure would be so beneficial for the other factors in his golden circle: the external account, the strength of the dollar, the basis for new private-sector enterprises like Macquarie Group, and so on.

I have observed that we live in a world where huge amounts of privately owned and controlled funds and financial paper sweep across civilisation, outside the control of such protective institutions as the American Federal Reserve, the International Monetary Fund, or the Bank for International Settlements at Basle. We have seen them smash the South-East Asian nations' boom in the 1990s through speculative raids against their currencies. Australia's vulnerability to the currency hedge funds has resided in a chronic tendency to spend abroad more than it saves. This originally took the form of Australian governments running large public-sector deficits. But as public-sector financial discipline has improved, the 'budget deficit' has become less of a problem for us than it once was. Its place has been taken by a private-sector deficit: the big commercial banks borrowing short-term funds abroad to finance such things as housing booms.

This spill of bank short-term borrowing abroad came to settle—give or take a percentage point—at about 6 per cent of national income. In the mid-1990s, Paul Keating figured out that once he had raised superannuation payments from 9 per cent of incomes to 15 per cent—that is, by six percentage points—he would have solved Australia's vulnerability to the 'current account deficit' because our banks' propensity to borrow that extra 6 per cent would be matched roughly by the domestic workforce's propensity to save an extra 6 per cent of pay: the borrowing spill abroad would diminish to the point of near-irrelevancy.

Keating, with his ultimately heightened grasp of economic dynamics, would usually accompany this point with a warning about our terms of trade that ran along these lines: because, unit for unit, the prices for goods we sell abroad—coal, iron ore, wool, cattle, wheat, and so on—had for years run ahead of the unit prices of goods we bought from abroad—television sets, computers, electronics of all kinds (the prices for most of which were actually falling), we had what was seen as a superior terms of-trade position. That is, the prices of things we sold were rising considerably faster than the prices of thing we bought. This was a gain in real income, and it salved our tendency to push too many Australian dollars abroad into the hands of the raiders.

But how long could we continue to rely on having our external account problem solved by this considerable relative strength in our export prices? Who could predict that? How many points of growth might China slow down per year in a switch of attention to 'green' matters, or to household matters? Say the oft-talked about recession in America did occur, due to the rot in mortgage capital, perhaps exacerbated by a slump in national confidence stemming from a sudden realisation that the United States, for all its glory, had been beaten by a collection of mad mullahs? Such geo-political factors as these could switch the international balance of demand and supply in such a way as to swiftly and adversely turn around Australia's favourable 'terms of trade'.

Keating liked to point out the consequences of such a development with a scenario running as follows. A group of international currency traders are sitting around a coffee shop in Amsterdam swapping notes. 'I suddenly find I'm holding more Australian dollars than I usually do,' says one. 'Do you want to buy some?' 'Funny you should mention that,' says another. 'I've got a load more than I want. 'Time to launch a selling blitzkrieg here, boys, don't you think?' says another.

It turns out that Keating has been somewhat premature in the 'hedge traders' bazaar' aspect of his concern about an excess of Australian dollars floating abroad. Australia's favourable terms of trade have lasted a lot longer than his musings allowed, for reasons not apparent when he first indulged in them. But something like this is certainly not fanciful if the international terms of trade do switch against Australia, and in the next two years we will know if that is going to happen. The only way to guard against his Amsterdam coffee shop scenario is to increase domestic savings, to generate a better match between international buying and selling of the local currency. And the only practical way to expect this to occur as a profound step would be to lift the percentage of saved wages going into pension funds.

Paul Keating is right about the climacteric threat. We are psychologically vulnerable because the greater part of our population has not experienced a period of history when the prices of our export staples do not go on rising inexorably. But such periods are well and truly there within historical memory and, if they occur in a setting of a chronic excess of external short-term debt over credit, the impact here would be devastating. This is why Australia suffered so badly in the Great Depression.

The prospect of such a disaster was not the primary thing in the mind of the Treasury team working away on the 15 per cent pension-fund prescription under the fascinated gaze of treasurer Keating and then prime minister Keating. The main impellent of the team was the conclusion that if Australia was going to make a policy feature of workers' pension funds, 15 per cent was what was required to ensure a comfortable old age.

It was Keating and his recent exposure to what the international hedge funds as a group could do when in full flight that conjured up the golden circle and the Amsterdam coffee house scenario: he had witnessed the sack of so recently lauded 'miracle economies' such as Thailand and Indonesia. He wanted to achieve equilibrium between the domestic balance and the external balance, which was what a 15 per cent savings ratio could bring. One of the benefits of this would be a resilient dollar in any 'terms of trade' setting—and not only this, but a low and stable interest-rate setting à la Switzerland, where interest-rate obsession ceases to become the little-understood but nonetheless incessant stuff of politics that it is in Australia.

I discovered through my enquiries that, when the Howard government came to power, the Treasury duly presented the fruits of their years of domestic savings-ratio research labours to treasurer Costello. The Treasury people were amazed to find that Costello wanted to go no further with this work. Was Costello an intelligent man? I asked. Yes, they said, he was a very intelligent man. What was his reasoning, then, for cutting this thoroughly reasoned scheme off at the 9 per cent at which it stood on Keating's departure?

Treasury's answer to me, to the question of why their own work on savings and superannuation was put on ice, was that the matter was 'political'. Political? I have long been aware that I would have been a disastrous Treasury man. I could not have shut up about the Treasury's work towards the 15 per cent workers' pension fund that went on for years and came to a sudden end. A good Treasury man can keep his mouth closed not only about the work, but also about speculation as to why a new government should suddenly terminate it, worthy though it had seemed.

I was left to draw my own inferences. It was difficult not to conclude that Peter Costello and John Howard had chopped the work off at the knees because it had become Paul Keating's darling, and that they had done so out of political spleen, distrust of the unions, and a tactical desire to keep budget tax-cuts uncomplicated.

In the years immediately after the 1996 election, Paul Keating went cap in hand to both the coalition and his own party, telling the story of the golden circle policy and the benefits that would accrue from it, and stressing that a quick movement to the 15 per cent savings ratio for pension funds was required. So much for the supposed innate arrogance of the man. There was an almost child-like trust on Keating's part that his peers would grasp his points. But his reasoned humility counted for nothing. Powerful people turned away; they simply did not want to know about it.

Chapter 10

Prejudice and Betrayal

'To him that hath, more shall be given …'
–Percy Bysshe Shelley

By 2006, the singular mix of coalition antipathy and Labor Party apathy and confusion towards the Keating–Kelty industrial pensions accord had taken hold. The passage of time had become a sorry fact of life for all connected with original hopes and ambitions. But, though stuck at 9 per cent, the endeavour was still alive, and its supporters waited like northern Tories in the first half of the 18th century for some descendant of the king over the water to return.

Some two years before the defeat of the Howard government, I asked Gerard Noonan, chair of the JUST industry superannuation fund, to think back to the period of changeover from Keating to the Howard–Costello ascendancy. He told me that, among his fellow industrial-fund executives, there had been a real fear that Howard and Costello would not only decline to progress with Keating's plan, but would scrub government support for the infant industrial-funds movement altogether. Howard and Costello had shown their antagonism to what they liked to call the union pension funds, and their preference was to not have them at all. Noonan said that three things saved them from this fate.

'At the point of change of government back in 1996, the incoming government was right on the cusp of opting out of the industrial pension-funds business. They would do this by ending, for ideological reasons, the superannuation guarantee charge which is the government's part in the business.

'But when they looked at this, they realised that the industrial super business had reached a size where the pain in dismantling it would be politically costly. It was a close-run thing, really. Had the industry movement been a little smaller, we could have been gone. So that is the first reason. We had reached a politically critical size.

'The second reason was that the more enlightened heads of employers' organisations had been impressed with the way Kelty and Keating had got the funds going as a mix of worker, employer, and government contribution. They wanted to preserve what was happening. Bert Evans, at the helm of the Metal Trades Industry Association, had been through years of cooperation with Keating, Kelty, and Hawke to hold the wages accord in place. He was about to retire, but he saw the constructive climate the industry funds were creating, and wanted them sustained.

'The Metal Trades Industry Association was about to merge with the Australian Chambers of Manufactures to become the top industrial organisation, under the title Australian Industry Group, and Heather Ridout was soon to become chief executive of the new group. She, too, backed the new pension funds, and made workers' pension funds and retirement incomes a prominent part of the Australian Industry Group's agenda.

'In the face of this sympathy and support from the employers' side, Howard and Costello, only tenuously in power at this point, were not about to ditch the Keating scheme altogether. But this brings me to the third point: at least as important a factor as strength of employers' support for the funds was the contempt of the coalition for any independent enterprise run by unions. The way they saw industrial history in Australia was that the industry funds would go the way of previous efforts to encourage union-run financial enterprise—namely, into what they saw as a miasma of rorts and boondoggles. Leave the workers' pension thing alone, and it would soon go the way of similar endeavours, was what they thought; but, for heaven's sake, don't commit to increase Commonwealth contributions to it.

'So, in an atmosphere of mild contempt from the new government, the workers' pension fund movement was allowed to survive as it was.

'Then, for a time, it became an object of almost benign attention from the traditional managers and guides of superannuation in Australia such as AMP, Colonial, MLC, BT Financial, Commonwealth Bank, ANZ Bank, Westpac Bank, and so on, the so-called retail funds. Because at first our industrial funds felt themselves not in a position to provide the kind of after-care needed once the worker was ready to leave work, we tended to hand our retiring people on to the commercial funds to get themselves set up with such things as allocated pensions that required actuarial work.

'But once we knew we were going to survive and we grew in confidence, we decided it was silly for us not to do this stuff ourselves. And that ended a cosy affair. Ever since then, there has been antipathy between ourselves and the commercial funds, and Costello has taken every opportunity he can to let the commercial funds have a go at us. But that has been an irony in favour of us. History for us, in the last ten years or so, has been a case of that which does not kill us makes us stronger.'

'Can you give me some examples?'

'Well, once we stopped handing our retirees over to the commercial funds for after-care, it became an increasing complaint on the part of the commercial funds that we weren't giving employees within our ambit a reasonable choice as to which fund they joined. Costello was only too happy to take this up. He arranged legislation which required employees starting off in superannuation with a company to be given a clear choice as to where they wanted to go—into an industrial fund or into a commercial fund, that is, the AMP-type fund and the bank funds.'

This legislation, known as the Choice of Fund Act, was passed in 2004 and came into effect on 1 July 2005. It required an employee entering 9 per cent superannuation to be given a choice between an industry fund run by people like Gerard Noonan and a commercial fund run by people like AMP or the banks.

'It was actually more complicated than that' said Gerard. 'It required the employee to be given a choice between a minimum of five different funds. And the choice had to be presented objectively by business. And, in fact, the Democrats spotted the political vulnerability in this. They saw that, for small business, the task of taking an employee through a minimum choice of five different funds, explaining all this to them and then doing the paperwork could become quite a burden.

'Nevertheless, the government went ahead with this so-called Choice of Fund legislation—the assumption on the part of the government and the commercial funds being that, given the choice, most employees would go for the AMPs, Commonwealth Banks, Westpac Banks, etc. So that the industry funds movement would be cut smartly down to size, and there was still this hope on the part of the conservatives that, given this kind of choice, the industrial-funds movement might wither on the vine.'

'Did you think you might?'

'I must say that, given this constant choice and opportunity for the commercial funds to present their wares, I thought we might be in danger. But, much to everyone's surprise, the reverse happened. We went for some intensive television advertising that played to people's intelligence, and the result was surprising. Instead of us losing in the recruitment of members, it was the other side that lost. And this can be shown in the flow of funds into the industry funds during the period.

'To know you were simply staying where you were, a fund should get 9 per cent of contributions. That was par. Now, despite the fact that the government was doing everything it could to assist the commercial funds vis-à-vis ourselves—things like special superannuation deposit accounts for the banks, where people could simply put their money in a special bank account and it would be treated as a super fund—despite all this, it became apparent that we were growing at between 20 and 25 per cent a year throughout this period, which meant that the government's choice-of-fund ploy was working in reverse to their desires.

'For the government-cum-commercial fund camp, it was a failure. What was actually happening was that there was a flow into the industry funds from elsewhere, in spite of everything. The pressure that came on the government to swing things in favour of our opposition was very, very strong. The Choice of Fund Act made it easier for a person to leave one fund and go to another, and there was this expectation when it came into effect that people who had just come into the industry funds without thinking much about it would move to the commercial funds. But the movement was the other way—towards us.'

'Where else has the bias against the industry funds appeared?'

'Well, another example has been the goings-on in the Senate. We are now into a second enquiry in the Senate where the aim seems to be to produce legislation requiring greater prudential investment for the industry funds—to put upon them a tiered-capital basis like the banks. To us, this would be an unnecessary burden on our capital, and we resisted it. The chief protagonist in this is a senator from the coalition side, Grant Chapman, whose aim seems to be to do whatever he can to prevent the industrial funds from operating as effectively as they can. That is so, in our view at least.'

'What motivates Senator Chapman?'

'It seems to me to be a strong personal animus between Grant Chapman and Garry Weaven, the man seen as the doyen of the industry-funds movement. There have been some quite tough exchanges between Weaven and Chapman.'

'Gerard, we have gone through the story of the funds' survival from the threat of death in infancy. At what stage would you say that your funds passed a critical mass point, and not only saw ahead of them a viable life but became a substantial institution in the system?'

Noonan saw the critical-mass point as at the beginning of the century. By that stage there were thousands of different funds, and their atomised state signalled danger. A process of consolidation began to signal maturity and safety.

'Funds began consolidating, to become typically between $5 billion and $20 billion in size,' he said. 'There was a kind of gravitational pull towards critical mass and hence towards consolidated funds standing as significant financial institutions. With that came the emergence of things like the Members' Equity Bank, now a fully capitalised bank which has come out of the funds movement. This is a bank that provides everything from allocated pensions through to debt collection.'

AS TIME WORE ON, Peter Costello could see that, despite his truncation of the Keating schema, the industry funds were going to power on sufficiently to leave a lasting legacy for Keating. He decided to come up with his own monument in the development of superannuation. His scheme, announced in the budget of May 2006 to much upper-middle-class excitement, exempted Australians aged 60 or more from tax on their end benefits, as long as the benefits were paid from a taxed superannuation fund. There was a transition period up to the end of June 2007 during which people would be able to put up to a million dollars into their super funds without tax penalty. In this transition period, small-business people would be able to sell their business and put the proceeds into superannuation without attracting a penalty. Michaela Anderson, from the Association of Superannuation Funds of Australia, thought the provision was very generous.

But the language surrounding this substantial move by Peter Costello reeked of unconscious irony and conscious sarcasm. In introducing the legislation, Costello thanked the Labor opposition for their 'belated' support for his initiatives:

the 'belated' was rich, coming from a man who cut out the residuary of the Keating scheme. And to those who understood what had happened, Costello's spruiking of his legislation articulated irony. It said a good deal about the then existing state of intellectual rigour in the Labor party on the matter that he was not challenged.

In the 2006 budget, Costello also introduced further income-tax cuts, reducing marginal tax rates at the top of the income scale, and lifting the rates' thresholds at the lower end. At a café lunch after the 2006 Commonwealth budget, I asked Keating what he thought about the pension and tax reforms.

'Paul,' I said, 'I watch the current affairs programs, and I find the commentators are now full of praise for legislation that Costello is bringing on to boost superannuation. Hasn't he rather stolen your thunder?'

Keating proceeded to take the Costello ploys apart.

'What Costello has finally done on superannuation is nothing like I was aiming at, because there is such a small proportion of our population who can afford to take advantage of his scheme,' he said. 'If you're aiming at the wealthy, you can make increased superannuation sound like a lot. But it's like playing with the top personal rate of tax: cut the rate from 47 per cent to 45 per cent or even 40 per cent, and this sounds dramatic. But in terms of total community incomes it is not very much, because there's next to nobody up there. It's the same with super: if you confine 9 per cent super, or 15 per cent for that matter, to the higher-income brackets, you are not doing very much because not many people are wealthy.

'But if you have a 9 per cent mandatory system of superannuation that extends to lower-income earners and middle-income earners, you are talking about more than a trillion dollars at full flow. At 15 per cent, you are talking about one-and-a-half trillion dollars [at that point]. You are safe from whatever the world can throw at you.

'What Costello has done says that the Liberal Party does not want to extend support for superannuation to the majority of the people. They want tax concessions for the top end of town or for those people who have had it for a century in the public service.

'A conservative friend of mine who was at the top of the US administration said to me: "You have the strangest conservative party in the world. If you cut a line through conservatives in all of the rest of the world, you would find one thing they'd all say they stood for, and that would be thrift.

'"But in Australia, you have had the unlikely event of a Labor government virtually conscripting the workforce to put 9 per cent of income away as savings, and then comes a conservative government succeeding Labor and declining to take the opportunity to build on that 9 per cent and, what's more, wanting to damage it. I find this very strange and hard to understand," he said.

'What Costello is doing is re-opening the lurky parts of superannuation. He is essentially saying to anyone who can afford to pay big voluntary amounts each year into their superannuation accounts, please take advantage of this. You can have your lump sum free of charge. You can change one asset for another. And that's largely all that's going to happen. But that is not what we want. That is not saving in an economic sense. We want to advance superannuation on the basis of universality and equity. That is what my march towards 15 per cent was about, apart from its huge economic significance.

'What the conservatives have done shows the confusion

and contradiction in their policy thinking. We gave them an economy high enough in productivity to begin producing big budget surpluses. These surpluses invited tax cutting, and they had a choice about how they went about that tax cutting. I wanted it in the form of contribution to super funds. If they had done that in 2006, then that alone in one swoop would have lifted 9 per cent universal superannuation to 12 per cent.

'But, no. They couldn't bring themselves to do that. They did a bit on superannuation for the top end, and released the rest as ordinary tax cuts. The tax cuts were of sufficient volume to bring them into conflict with the Reserve Bank, and we had another interest increase. If they had lifted universal super to 12 per cent instead, their tax cuts would have been saved and there would have been no conflict with the Reserve Bank. And the stupid thing about all this politically is that they got no thanks for their tax cuts.'

'Let's assume that the budget surpluses keep rolling because the economy is in such good condition,' I said. 'What's the chance of them putting the next round of tax cuts into universal super?'

'Oh, I don't think they'll do that because, frankly, they don't want the workers managing money. They want their friends to be doing that. If you have a pinstripe suit on and a Liberal Party ticket in your pocket, then you are one of the chosen to run the savings of the rest of us.

'But if you are the trustee of an industry fund, you cannot be relied upon, according to Howard and Costello, to wisely invest the money. Even though we know now that the industry funds are the leading providers of returns.

'The economics of it—the drive towards counter-balancing the wash of Australian dollars abroad with domestic savings—is not spoken of anymore. The reason that it is not spoken of is that it is so hard to deal with unless you do what I was doing—drive for one-and-a-half trillion dollars to close the golden circle.'

'Paul, suppose it could be taken up again. Is there another Bill Kelty out there who could act as he did as a go-between with the unions?'

Paul Keating had now entered a stage where he was prepared to indulge in continuously varying calculations on the pension funds in order to keep the flame alive. In these depths of despond, emphasis on the grand economic relevance of it all subsided. This was to return when Kevin Rudd looked like gaining power. But now calculation of proportions became an obsession in a sad vigour towards a diminished end:

'I've talked to Greg Combet, the secretary of the ACTU about this. When Bill Kelty and I started we did it first industrially, without the government. That's perhaps what we've got to turn back to. It took Kelty and me from 1985 to 1990 to get the first 3 per cent superannuation into awards paid to employees by employers, in lieu of cash.

'Now, if we could get the ACTU to meet with the Business Council of Australia and the Australian Industry Group, and get on the table a proposition that in the next 5 per cent wage round we pay 4 per cent of cash wages and the remaining 1 per cent of that wages-lift paid as savings into the existing superannuation funds, so that over the course of a four-year agreement we would get 4 per cent away to super—that would be something.

'What could happen is that a sufficiently large minded employers' group would say to the unions, we'll give half a per cent and you give half a per cent each in lieu of cash, and we would build that year upon year for four years. That would get us to 13 per cent of workers' incomes in industrial superannuation. It took us all these years to get to nine. What is wrong with taking the next four years of an industrial agreement to get to 13? Then in the next round of industrial agreement we would get to the desired 15, and stop there.'

'What would the government do?'

'Well, if it were this government, the Howard government, it wouldn't do anything, which would be a big mistake because the way I had the government's co-payments set up, they became an important part of budgetary machinery—of economic management. What this government would say, though, is that further employers' contribution to industry super funds is a further tax on employers. But that, of course, is nonsense. It is not a tax on employers so long as it is paid in agreement instead of wages that would otherwise have been paid.

'But the trouble is that there is a villainy within the employers' heartland who won't put it this way, who would come and say, look, this is shocking, the unions are now seeking to put another 4 per cent away in savings, and this is just a disguised tax on employers. It would need the more enlightened of employers to come in and say, that is nonsense. If we were paying the full 1 per cent super, it would be 1 per cent super and 4 per cent wages instead of 5 per cent wages.

'Any country has got to get very lucky to get anything like the 9 per cent that we got before progress was cut down. Having got there, it is not such a huge thing to get to the 15. But it's a huge thing for the economy. That is where we must aim: at 15 per cent we are right, done. And our economy will be unique.

'Of course, you have to be very unlucky to get to the 9 per cent and then have a government walking away from it.

'If I let myself, this is why I get so exasperated with this Howard government. Sometimes I can't believe it: they provide a direct tax cut and then spend the rest of the year worrying about whether the bank will raise interest rates to counter the tax cut's effect. If they could have gone on paying it into workers' super it would have been so simple, once Bill Kelty and I had got it going, and everyone would have been better off. Something very good and clever did happen here to get us to the 9 per cent.'

'And you think it's prejudice—the reason that it didn't go on?'

'Prejudice and betrayal.'

'What is needed for the government to get back in it?'

'It needs someone to rise above party lines and say, look, this is not that hard to do. Let's do it.'

'What do you make of the contradictions we are getting from Peter Costello these days?' I asked. 'By that, I mean that we have his warning—which is fair enough—that by 2040, instead of having five workers for every one of the aged population, we are only going to have two-and-a-half. But then he infers that, as long as you have any sort of a surplus in the budget, you can cut taxes and/or spend?'

Keating answered: 'Well, these remarks about intergenerational transfers are all well and good, and to be applauded. But what is not genuine is a policy of running the surplus on empty—that is to say, having the most nominal surplus when you have had a poultice of revenue—and spending all the revenue so that you end up with the surplus needle hovering above empty again at the end of the year. The true surplus has been frittered away over a decade on a scale that someone like me could only have dreamt of. And the economic cost of not going on with those steps of mine, of putting 3 per cent ordinary taxpayers' incomes away into the super funds that I established, has been profound. I've had calculations done on what the further 3 per cent for pension funds provided for in my budgeting would be worth now had they stayed in Costello's budgets, and the answer is between $400 billion and $500 billion.

'So we lost that decade of accumulation. But instead of righting the wrong, however late, and starting to put some of this into their superannuation—as his own figures suggest that they should—what does he do? He says, if you've got a million to spare before 30 June 2007, put it into superannuation. But on the quite different question of long-term pension adequacy, you can stay on 9 per cent. It's quite contradictory.

'I don't care who does it. I don't care if it's the Labor Party or the Liberal Party. Whoever gets super to 15 per cent first—say first to 12 per cent and then to 15 per cent—gets the tick from me.'

'It's rather unlike Peter Costello to be so inconsistent, don't you think?'

'Yes, well. The answer lies in the fact that they hate industry fund-type superannuation, you see. Despite the fact that the industry funds have shown themselves to have been exemplary, and that employer organisations make up half the trustees, they still don't want industry funds. They have this ideological obsession against industry funds and super contributions in lieu of tax cuts.

'They'll only let people add to superannuation voluntarily, and that is by taking up the provision that the treasurer offered at the last budget. If you or I have a million to spare, then you put it in and that's a good thing. But if you are out there chasing the garbage trucks and all you've got is the present 9 per cent, then you get no more.

'And to change this would be just so easy to do. If they want to avoid the unions they can just call in a suitable set of employer organisations. And look, do this—'

A Montblanc fountain pen flashed from his pocket, and we seized the back of one of the cafe's menu sheets. I held the sheet while, with strong urging from Keating, the pen charged across the page. We returned again to the suppositional slicing of contributions from industry and unions. This time, the equivalent contributions from the unions and the employees had become 0.37 per cent of the wage increase each year, instead of the previous 0.50 per cent.

To me, a great part of the appeal of the Keating pensions scheme was the way it operated as part of Budget strategy. But at this point in 2006 he was prepared to let the arm of government slide from the scheme in order to keep the arithmetic within the bounds of hope. His struggle with frustration was going to go further in a boilover at a superannuation conference in 2007 where, in despair, he indicated a readiness to hand all of the initiative over to union aggression. In 2006, however, he was still coming to terms with the failure to advance the pensions scheme in politics.

'Should this step be hard to take?' Paul asked rhetorically. 'No. Let's have it at its most basic. If politicians don't want tax cuts in it, they need not. They need only approach a suitably large employers' group and the matter would run from there. Any treasurer worth his salt should be capable of doing that. Just get 'em in, say this is what we want you to do. Other employer groups and other workers would fairly quickly join in.

'Instead of this, what's this treasurer doing? He's pumping cash into the system so that the Reserve Bank has to take it out in interest rates.

'The Labor Party hasn't been any better so far. It really is a strange situation, given the intergenerational change situation which everybody knows is coming.'

Politics as a generator of political change seemed to have stopped working here, I thought. When the policy of an outgoing party's government has been dropped or throttled down by the incoming party's government, one usually can rely on the Westminster system to ensure that a dialectic grind continues.

Unless the policy is discredited, like slavery, the processes of government and opposition will keep it alive until the system gives it the chance to rise again under the ultimate return of the defeated party, or become modified into something else in the longer life of the ascendant party. But for more than a decade in opposition, Labor's part in the question of the survival or growth of the three-way co-payments industry superannuation funds question was quite remote. And so the matter stayed, at best, suspended, not yet two-thirds of the way there.

Chapter 11

The Process of Forgetting

When Keating's government lost office in March 1996, Kim Beazley immediately succeeded Keating as leader of the parliamentary Labor Party. The former prime minister heard nothing from his former colleagues in the years after his defeat, so he began seeking out senior members of the Labor front bench to stress the importance of maintaining the ACTU's unity with the party on industrial superannuation, and of taking the pension contribution through to 15 per cent of workers' pay. This was needed, he kept on explaining, not only to secure the comfort of workers in their old age, but also to secure current-account equilibrium for Australia in such a way as to protect us from currency predators. It was crucial for a variety of reasons, not just size of the ultimate pension, to secure the final six percentage points of the Keating plan.

But Keating's successors in Labor didn't want to know about the golden circle; they didn't want to try to understand what he was getting at. They put 'pensions and retirement' in the hands of an obscure Tasmanian senator who proceeded to build for Labor a pensions policy that was largely the opposite of Keating's creation.

John Lyons, a former editor of the *Sydney Morning Herald*, related in a *Bulletin* article how, after the 1996 election, a prominent Labor figure had told him he would cross the road when he saw Keating coming, 'rather than listen to another one of Keating's lectures about how the public didn't understand him'.

This says a great deal more about the senior ranks of the Labor Party in the decade after Labor's defeat than it does about Paul Keating. It says that the people selected to lead Labor after Keating did not bother to understand what Keating and his policies were all about: they did not bother to look at the widespread dynamics of the pension-fund policy that Keating was seeking to preserve, and thus did not bother to understand how Australia now had a stock market that was far ahead of Singapore and Hong Kong both in terms of turnover and market capitalisation, and second in Asia only to Japan.

They did not bother to understand how the nation had accrued the largest pool of investment funds in Asia and the fourth largest in the world; did not bother to understand how we were increasing our share of the global foreign-exchange market while the rest of the Asia-Pacific was losing theirs; did not bother to understand how we had overtaken Switzerland as a foreign-exchange market; did not bother to understand how the Australian dollar was now the sixth-most-traded currency in the world. Most of all, the leaders of the Australian Labor Party did not try to understand how all this could get much better if Keating's work was continued, taking us to a place of astonishing market depth and sophistication.

Under Kim Beazley and Simon Crean's leadership, a

disdain for Paul Keating's record as Labor leader was allowed to develop within the federal parliamentary party. As part of this, any attempt to assess Keating's contribution was also disdained.

There is a tragedy in the ALP's continuing ignorance about what Keating had set up for this country. We should despair that, up to the very point of Labor's assumption of power in late 2007, so many in the party showed the same old primitive grasp of financial economics, and a continuing ignorance of their former leader and the financial reforms he created.

It's a telling measure of how far the official party process of forgetting went that, in writing this book about the extraordinary changes to the Australian economy in the Keating period, I have found it necessary to devote the second part of this book to the fate of Keating's legacy.

CONSIDERABLE RESPONSIBILITY for the misunderstanding of Keating's legacy lies in the innocent stupidity of one Nick Sherry, a Tasmanian Labor frontbencher. The reader might find this assessment of an individual MP rather heavy-handed, especially given the man's history during this time. Let me state that I intend no personal malice towards Sherry. I see his place in this story as largely another example of the operations of Shakespearean chance: history is strewn with examples of a huge enterprise being thwarted by the actions of confused small players, and this is just another one of them.

After the 1996 election, Sherry, a senator who had been a parliamentary secretary in the Keating government, became a member of Labor's federal parliamentary shadow cabinet. When he took over the shadow portfolio of retirement incomes and savings in 2001, the official contribution to pensions was at 9 per cent of income, the level it had reached while Keating was in office. The Howard government had decided not to continue with Labor's sliding scale of increases in contributions: the figure of 9 per cent had no status in logic other than that it was the applicable rate when Keating was defeated. Nevertheless, Sherry appears to have accepted the figure as if it had a self-supporting logic akin to $E=MC^2$.

While Keating was fighting to have the rationale of his pension and investment work restored within Labor policy, Sherry declared that anything more than 9 per cent would be too much, on the grounds that it was 'too costly'. In such a way was federal Labor policy formed; a mindless benchmark of 9 per cent became the cornerstone of Labor 'retirement incomes and savings' policy.

One should not sheet home the blame for this perfidy to Senator Sherry alone. The fact that Sherry was able to run his policy as Labor's official pensions policy indicates two things about federal Labor in opposition. Once a member of caucus was ensconced under factional backing within the shadow cabinet, they could often do more or less what they wanted regarding policy in their portfolio area. Second, neither Simon Crean nor Kim Beazley appreciated what Paul Keating had achieved, and was still trying to achieve, at the time of his defeat. Either that, or they were so consumed by factional territorialism and in-fighting that they failed to defend Keating's intellectual and political legacy.

Either way, this critical area of opposition policy was left at the mercy of a man who had no real concept of the glories of Keating's savings policy before and after the 1996 election, and of what it had delivered to Australia's economic and social structure. Labor could have ridden out these barren years in opposition with a policy that aimed to spell out the connection between the industrial pension funds' growth and the growth of Australia as a world financial power way above the size of its population and the strength of its primary and secondary industries. Having hammered this argument into the electorate's consciousness, Labor could then have painted the further benefits to be gained by extending contributions to superannuation. They could have taken up the golden circle theory, which would have been, intellectually, a very respectable proposition. For starters, they could have defined the golden circle—that is, 'the line that runs through rising household savings to rising capital supply to rising international strength to stable interest rates, and back to rising household net wealth'. But no one recalled the theory.

The disconnection between Keating and Sherry is revealed in Sherry's speeches of the period. He liked to illustrate in a folksy way the correctness of the 9 per cent cap on contributions by bringing in Tasmanian characters who supposedly had no hope of finding another thousand dollars to add to their pension fund.

These tales were quite beside the point, because any progression in Keating's pension policy would not have required them to find the funds from their existing resources. Sherry not only demonstrated a complete misunderstanding of what Keating was about, and a lack of awareness of how Keating's savings ratio related to the country's external account, market liquidity, financial product growth and other things; he showed no appreciation of the surplus budgets that presented themselves to the Howard government in the years following the Australian productivity surge of the late 1990s.

Keating's savings-ratio progression would have fitted painlessly and seamlessly into the succession of Commonwealth budget surpluses. Payments to pension funds in lieu of tax cuts would have eliminated the necessity for Reserve Bank interest-rate rises to counter the stimulatory effects of tax cuts to consumers.

Let me invoke here the opinion of an outside observer, Terry Sweetman, a veteran newspaper columnist and former News Ltd editor who has no reason to take sides on the issue. After Sherry rejected a call by Keating to lift workers' pension fund contributions by six percentage points, Sweetman wrote in the *Courier-Mail*:

> That's a craven renouncement of the legacy of a far-sighted Labor scheme that, for the first time, offered all Australians at least the promise of self-funded retirement with dignity and a degree of comfort. The truth is that we've come a long way in a short time, but nobody (presently) on either side of politics has the will or the ticker to complete the journey. We now have one trillion locked away in super. But it could and should be more ... It's still a far cry from the $629,266 a couple needs to aspire to a comfortable retirement, or the $341,874 they need for a modest retirement income as calculated by Westpac and the Association of Superannuation Funds.
>
> Figures from the Association of Super Funds show a 40-year-old with 25 years left to work and earning an annual salary of $50,000 could expect to accumulate $250,000 under the 9 per cent contribution rate. At 12 per cent it would be $313,000 and at 15 per cent it could be $377,000. On a salary of $80,000 the respective savings would be $313,000, $398,000 and $483,000. On $110,000 a year the savings would be $409,000, $525,000 and $641,000 ...

> According to Sherry, Labor prefers to limit its superannuation ambitions to crafting policies that help those who missed out on the Costello superannuation reforms, although we get no details on how this would be done. The fact remains that the single most effective way of providing retirement security and equity must be to increase the ability of ordinary people to build their superannuation accounts.

Sweetman argued that an incremental increase in the contribution rate from 9 to 15 per cent over a period of about six years 'should not be beyond the reach of even the most financially cautious Labor government'. He went on to chide the opposition: 'Labor should have learned the hard way over recent elections that there is no profit in me-too-ism and low-profile politics.'

In the long years of pain and frustration for Keating since Howard and Costello's chopping of his savings-ratio progression, Keating worked continually on papers and presentations to show why his scheme should not have been axed. But through all this he did not direct his attack at his former Labor caucus colleagues. That is, not until Sherry began to go public in 2007 with an aggressive rebuttal of the Keating scheme, saying there was 'no way' Labor would go back to the Keating super plan:

> It's clearly out of the question because the money's been spent elsewhere. At the end of the day there's no way Labor's going to back the [Keating] plan. We have important other priorities.

From a former caucus and ministerial colleague, this was

tantamount to a public betrayal. Keating promptly used an address to a meeting of superannuation fund executives on the Gold Coast to rebuke Sherry. In a question from the floor, he was asked about statements by both Nick Sherry and Peter Dutton, the Howard government's assistant treasurer, that they would not revisit the possibility of introducing the 15 per cent contribution.

Keating answered: 'Yes, well, they're dead ordinary, these guys. It amounts to a failure of the imagination. Do they think the 9 per cent or the one trillion got us to where we are now because of affordability? When they say "affordable", just remember what they're saying. They're talking about a government—the [Howard] government—that spends all of the surplus all of the time. It keeps the surplus near enough on empty after it's had these massive revenues from 15 years of growth. It is leaving the national savings we should be getting from these revenues on the cabinet table each year, to be plundered by a group of greedy spending ministers. Are the potential national savings best dealt with in this way? Or are they best moved to individual Australians' national super accounts and preserved to age 60?'

Keating's questioner went on: 'Shadow treasurer Wayne Swan did say last month that Labor now supported the 15 per cent contribution. But Sherry went on the record as saying the issue was still dead. What do you make of that?'

Keating: 'Well, you don't expect Dutton, the coalition spokesman on superannuation, to be out there barracking for workers' superannuation, do you? But this view of affordability that Sherry puts, this accountancy approach, is a strange thing. This is not an accountancy matter. The budget is in structural surplus. Increase in pension fund is affordable. Do you pay it into the government's Future Fund, as they seem to want to do? No. Do you pay it back as tax cuts? Yes. But as tax cuts paid on the individual taxpayer's behalf into his superannuation savings account. You know, it should not take a lot of grey matter to work that out.'

Questioner: 'Given that, 11 years ago, Labor was the party of super, what advice would you give Wayne Swan and Nick Sherry for regaining that title?'

Keating: 'Well, I've been encouraged by Swan's remarks. As amazing as it sounds, he has been the first person to mention the 15 per cent in the federal Labor Party in 11 years. But if I was Kevin Rudd I'd run Sherry out, frankly. He's the Labor spokesman for superannuation, but in my opinion he will bring not two cents worth of value to working people in superannuation. Labor's got to pay on results. And if the Labor Party doesn't look after the interests of ordinary working men and women, who will?'

Questioner: 'So what happens now: how do we get over the 9 per cent?'

Keating: 'A lot of the top-up can happen industrially. The Liberal Party has been so squarely against the working people getting the best deal. And the Labor Party has been so hopeless … Why wait for those guys to get it for you now when they're not going to? You'd better go out and get it for yourselves industrially.'

As far as Keating was concerned, at this point the gloves were off. And, significantly, he was now publicly advocating that the union movement—indeed, workers themselves—should take up the challenge of reinstating the 15 per cent contribution as official Labor policy. This is a step beyond the conversations reported in the previous chapter in which he was casting about to keep pension-fund progression a three-way deal that cooperatively involved employers, unions, and government. And those conversations were themselves a step beyond his desperately held hope of keeping budget-based government co-payments the lead factor in the pension-fund dynamic.

By the time of the Gold Coast meeting of superannuation fund executives in 2007, he had been provoked beyond his better judgement by the stupidity of others. As the next chapter of this book reveals, he does not really believe that the industrial pension movement has a future without government participation.

BACK IN SYDNEY, I sought out Gerard Noonan to discuss these developments. One of the questions I had been turning over in my mind concerned Nick Sherry's place in the Labor Party: whether he was making a one-man stand, or whether his views really reflected those of the party. Noonan confirmed to me that Sherry had a firm following, and reflected the party's traditional socialist views.

'Within the Labor movement, there is a significant strand of people—people on the left—who believe it is the responsibility of government to provide a pension for the working class, without its members having to go out and set about establishing their own pension schemes from their own resources,' he said. 'Nick Sherry is the leader of this group. His attitude, and the attitude of his followers, is that the more policies are devoted towards co-contribution pension funds such as have grown in the past 15 years, the more the government is being let off the hook, from doing what should be its job—what should be its job, at least, in the kind of polity that the socialists desire. Australian socialists have believed since the days of Sidney and Beatrice Webb that the workers' wages shouldn't be diverted in any form to building their own pension funds. Their wages should be fully available to them to meet their current needs.'

'But surely history has swept past this view,' I said. 'It is almost on a par with whether mine owners should or should not pay basic insurance for rugby league players in northern England. The solution was that the clubs became strong enough to set up their own insurance. Surely, with the workers' superannuation funds, the solution has become that, with the help of government tax policy, the workers are going to provide their own superannuation.'

'I agree with that.'

'You know, this is engrossing stuff. It says the old fundamental left wing is still alive and well in the Labor Party: the principle that the workers should have first call on government money. In the mid-1980s, the Labor left sat like stunned mullets as Keating took over the free-enterprise precepts of the Campbell Committee and used them as Labor policy. But now we are seeing a belated strike back from the left on pensions.'

Gerard Noonan said Nick Sherry knew he could not turn back the existing 9 per cent. But he wanted no advance on that. His focus was on those he saw as not being able to get the industrial pension. It was a Labor government's job to concentrate on looking after such people.

'And there are more like him in the party?'

'Certainly,' said Noonan. 'But since Paul made those remarks about the absence of policy initiative from the party itself, there has been Labor shadow treasurer Wayne Swan's statement, saying that he wanted to raise superannuation adequacy to 15 per cent by expanding the government's co-contribution scheme. He said it would be desirable over time for someone on average earnings to achieve 15 per cent total with a 3 per cent contribution of their own. Which might be done, for example, by relaxing the means test to better help those on middle incomes.'

'What do you think caused Swan to suddenly step up to the plate on this with a counterview to the Sherry faction within the party?'

'I think it's been a gradual shift of the ground. I think there have been enough people for enough time now arguing the case that it was a mistake by the coalition government to turn off the tap as they did. As intelligent politicians travel around, increasingly they are realising that Australia is seen in the world at large as a model on this. Swan has realised that, rather than make a limited target of himself, there is a value in being seen to be visionary. I think that Swan's political intelligence has picked that up. I think that he has seen that Keating is clearly going to be remembered for this triumph. But he has also seen that it is an unfinished symphony. I think he has seen that Sherry is not the person to do it. Sherry just doesn't have the visionary capacity to see that it is intrinsically a good thing for the country.'

We sat on the editorial floor of the *Sydney Morning Herald* in the Fairfax building on Sussex Street in Sydney. Brightly lit screens flashed and roiled like pin ball games in serried rows beside us. They were bringing Noonan instant intelligence from around the world.

He suggested we go for coffee to the Paradiso on the piazza below the Fairfax offices. Once out of the building and walking down towards the coffee shop, I became sentimental about the old *Sydney Morning Herald* when it resided in an ugly lump called The Bloody Tower (because so many journalists and editors had been sacked there). The Bloody Tower had been up-town on Sydney's Broadway where, years before, I had sat at a wooden table turned brown and greasy at the edges by successions of sweated palms and cigarettes. There was no air-conditioning, and in summer we had to open the windows to relieve the heat, exacerbated by too many bodies in too little space. Opening the windows was a dubious option because it let in gusts of grit from the chimneys of a brewery across the road. I told Gerard how fortunate he was.

We sat now at a table outside at the Paradiso under the shade and aroma of Australian peppercorn trees, with the breeze blowing up from Darling Harbour. We could look up Market Street into the masculine midriff of the city. I asked Gerard why he thought the Labor Party didn't give Keating his due.

'Why not acknowledge Keating in all this? Keating has almost single-handedly and tirelessly pursued a missionary role on the matter, talking to people about it and its relevance to the current account and our terms of trade and so on, until he suffers the humiliation of seeing their eyes glaze over.'

Noonan answered only indirectly: 'I can understand Keating's pain, his frustration over the party's failure to listen, and then suddenly out of the blue the party decides to take an interest in it. And that the interest should come not from the bloke who is supposed to be looking after super. But that's the way change occurs. It is unlikely to just rush up at you. But if there's someone there who knows he's right and is prepared to just work away, change will occur.

'I can now see a Labor government trading off on this pretty much as they did in the accord days: a tax cut for a wage restraint. Only it will be a tax cut going to the extent of 3 per cent into the superannuation savings ratio: then perhaps an employers' payment in lieu of a direct wage payment until the 15 per cent is reached. Fifteen per cent is not going to happen all at once.'

Gerard recommended a look at the national accounts, where one can see that consumption is on a runaway curve upwards, so that anything that improves savings over consumption is the preferable strategy.

'I think there's a very attractive proposition to be made out of this 15 per cent now, given that government is pulling in revenue big time. Swan gives me the impression of a man who wants to leave a legacy, and he can get himself the legacy of pushing the savings ratio now from 9 to 12 per cent then to 15 per cent, and that would be quite impressive.'

'And presumably he wouldn't have done this without consulting Rudd?' I said.

'That's right. So what you've got is the big-picture people like Rudd and Swan, and Gillard is an important player in all this now.

'And a man I see as an important sleeper in all of this is the man from the Beaconsfield mine disaster, the national secretary of the Australian Workers' Union, Bill Shorten. Bill is on the board of Australian Super, the biggest of the industrial funds—now a $22 billion fund which grows by the month. He has superannuation interests big time. He's about to become a member of parliament. He's about to become the Malcolm Turnbull on the Labor side. I would see him pushing the Wayne Swan side and giving leadership in the unions.'

As Noonan predicted, Shorten entered parliament as the Member for Maribyrnong after Labor's victory at the 2007 federal election. Kevin Rudd then shocked some members of his own party by overturning the tradition that caucus elect the ministry. In naming his cabinet, he ignored Keating's unsolicited suggestion that he should run Nick Sherry out of his old portfolio. Instead, he made him minister for superannuation and corporate law. Bill Shorten became parliamentary secretary for disabilities and children's services.

But, for the longer term, not much notice should be taken of Rudd's initial allocation of portfolios. His immediate task is to create a setting that will enable the government to correct the inflationary and external vulnerabilities that the Australian economy became exposed to in the course of the Howard years. This requires peace inside the party, and it also requires working through the $31 billion of tax cuts he pledged in answer to Howard and Costello's election promise. These are urgent issues. But it's a good bet that the golden circle will be resurrected, for reasons that Keating spells out in the next chapter, and that I take up in the last. Before the first Rudd government is through, it is going to require every bit of Keating economic philosophy it can lay its hands on.

Chapter 12

The Nag's Head Crisis

WHEN ELIZABETH I ESTABLISHED HER CHURCH OF ENGLAND, she proclaimed for England an apostolic descent from the original Peter coming down to the Archbishop of Canterbury and not to the Bishop of Rome. The big thing about Elizabeth was the vigour with which she prosecuted this change: for England, the seat of descent was Canterbury and not Rome; Canterbury was ordained by God in the English case. If you didn't like that, you had better watch out. So vigorous was her pursuit of Rome's supporters that, under the patronage of Philip of Spain, a special enclave formed in Flanders around the city of Douai to which English Roman Catholics could flee and where Philip endowed for them a Catholic university.

Hard at work on Philip's behalf were the Jesuits, whose job was to come up with an allegory to succour the souls of the English opting to stick with the Bishop of Rome. The Jesuits came up with a brilliant parable based on English piracy in the 16th century: it had become a peculiarly English exercise to run a string of nags with lanterns around their necks along beaches on stormy nights, so that sailors in the storm, seeing the lights, thought that there were other ships closer into the shore and hence that they were comfortable in deep water. Thus conned, ships sailed closer to shore and, as often as not, were wrecked on the beaches. So the Canterbury bishops became the nag's head bishops enticing souls to a bitter end, and those who managed to see through the deception of the nag's headlights would save their souls.

When John Howard and Peter Costello succeeded Paul Keating in office, the economic changes they made were few, the main one being to try to evict reformers like the industry pension funds from the bishoprics. By far the most important coalition initiative was to vigorously sow the message that Costello and Howard were the people ordained by God to manage the Australian economy. In this, they were aided by the post-Keating Labor opposition who seemed, for a long time, quite content to go along with them.

Howard and Costello were remarkably successful. Whenever people were asked in surveys who they thought were the superior economic managers, the majority said Howard and Costello, so that it became accepted as a statement of fact that, compared with the unholy Keating, Howard and Costello were undoubtedly Australia's ordained economic managers. It took some years for John Howard and Peter Costello to appear for what they actually were—nag's head bishops.

There were two false lights in particular that Howard and Costello dangled: one was that you could go on cutting taxes without following the Keating course of deferring some of the tax cuts into delayed spending via the industry pension funds. Increasingly, this tax policy was a nag's head leading to higher interest rates. The other, and perhaps ultimately more harmful, of the false lights was that as long as you started each year legislating for a surplus in the Commonwealth budget of around 1 per cent of national income, you were running a balanced economy. It was essential to keep stressing the virtue of the Commonwealth surplus and to ignore the fact that, if you ran such a surplus along with an increasing private-sector deficit, you were steadily unbalancing the economy.

In the past ten years, as private debt has spilled abroad, Australia's net international current-account deficit has grown from about $15 billion to more than $60 billion, while total net international debt due abroad has grown in that period from $200 billion to $600 billion. What this means in terms of market dramatics is that we have an external deficit that overwhelms Commonwealth budget surpluses in significance; that the Howard–Costello combination spent recent years pointing national attention in quite the wrong direction; that banks these days must fund a substantial part of their deposit base with short-term borrowings from abroad and thus that, suddenly, we find ourselves locked into an explosive United States money crisis. It means we have been led by a nag's head lantern into an international money crisis that very few understand and that most Australians have been encouraged to ignore.

SOON AFTER KEVIN RUDD won the 2007 elections, I visited Paul Keating once more, this time with a view to discussing the rapidly unfolding international crisis and its implications for the new Labor government. We met in the former prime minister's rooms, a short walk from Kings Cross. Keating has grasped at the possibility for hope in this once-charming part of Sydney. He is in a side street—once beautiful, now shabby-genteel—three streets down from the lacerated heart of the Cross. In selecting his entitlement for post-prime ministerial office space, he has renovated a floor in what used to be part of the stately home of Tusculum, off Macleay Street. The original house was designed by John Verge, who also designed Elizabeth House, and whom Keating believes was the best of the colonial architects.

Restored by fate having taken a kinder turn, with whatever damage his self-esteem had previously suffered now apparently healed, Keating pursues the intellectual interests that have nurtured him most—work, music, and his passion for collecting around great themes.

Our meeting took place in a large room dominated by columns of what he explained were the Tuscan order of Vignola (to match the memories of Tusculum). He said the settings should be described as a suite of columns that were a variation on the Corinthian. Where had they come from? I asked. They had come from Seven Oaks, he said, and I immediately thought of a plantation in the Old South. I had that wrong. They came from a place in Kent. Was the place in Kent the original Seven Oaks? Oh, yes. The suite had originated with a Mr Christie of Seven Oaks in 1799 and he, Keating, had bought it from someone in London. Within the pleasing inner space created by the columns, I sat facing a Louis XVI clock that was opulently ornate; its impression was of the rococo period, with just an early hint in its more austere base of the revolution in French art that was to come.

To my left, still in its recently opened wooden packing case, was a bust of Montesquieu, the French political philosopher of the Enlightenment. Close by, on the wall, was a painting of a young French couple circa 1810, with the woman's hair loosely combed and natural, and her clothes draped. If the young woman had lived perhaps 40 years earlier her clothing would have been ornate, and she would have worn a wig, the distance between the Louis XVI clock in front of me and the painting to my left marked the distance in French art and politics from romanticism to the neo-classicism of the Empire.

Keating is a stage star. He is still a political figure, but an extraordinary one: he ranges above party status.

'I am wrapping up my book, Paul,' I said, 'at a point where I find you a social lion. The human comedy being what it is, the musical—*Keating!*—has lifted you from the dark night of the soul and left you free to do almost whatever you want. Such are your achievements on policy in Australia, you know, you could be, if you wanted, a Henry Kissinger roaming the world giving lectures for fees. The rest of the world has been much more deeply impressed by your workers' pension fund achievements than we have here. You could name a high price internationally.'

'No, there's no point in that,' said Keating. 'I am already involved in an investment banking business, and mergers and acquisitions are our staple, and that's interesting. There's a lot of cleverness in it; I enjoy that. And there's an honest dollar to be earned in that. On public speaking, I've only just recently had a European governments' invitation to address provisioning of pensions, and I took that up. I still remain on the international advisory board of the China Development Bank, which is the largest policy bank in China. I keep busy.'

'Events of late hand you a moral victory, Paul—on the industry pension-funds matter and the spill abroad of private-sector credit. So when do you see it as an appropriate time for the Rudd government to get back to making extra payments into pension funds in lieu of tax cuts—to get back on the path again towards 12 per cent leading on to 15 per cent of average-incomes pension?'

Keating then began what was to be an extraordinary off-the-cuff dissertation on government in a world whose leader, whose centre—namely the USA—had let the side down. Gone was the insistence on his immediate imperative of a 15 per cent pensions ratio; in its place was a balanced advance in *realpolitik*. Rudd's first priority, he said, was to bring overall national spending back into a better balance with overall national saving, in order to quell the infection from abroad. This was going to require budgeting towards a surplus of 2 to 3 per cent of GDP, rather than the Howard–Costello performance of 1 per cent of GDP, and in a setting where Rudd had had to match the coalition in an election poker game with $31 billion in tax cuts. But once this was worked through, the movement by steps to a 15 per cent pension was imperative.

'Living to 90 is not now uncommon,' said Paul. 'People's expectations about how long they will live are changing dramatically: people who thought they might live to about 80 are now looking at 90. Thus our first priority—economic policy levers aside—is to cope with this change.

'When we first started setting our goals for government contribution to the industry-pension scheme back in the late 1980s, part of the reason we came up with 15 per cent of income was that that was what we thought we needed to accommodate the baby boomers who were already halfway through their working lives. So if you could front-load the system at 15 per cent, you would be able to give the baby boomers enough to retire on. This was apart from the other dynamics of 15 per cent that were coming to my mind—for economic stability, capital-market growth, external-account equilibrium.

'It turns out that that didn't happen. When Peter Costello and John Howard decided not to pay that second round of tax cuts as super in 1996 in their first budget, the baby boomers missed out. And the cost to the average baby boomer family of the loss of that superannuation from 1997–98 through to 2008—a period which encompassed the stock market boom—is probably about $200,000 per family.'

'Paul, there's a notion abroad that employers and employees can get together now and salary-sacrifice without the presence of government, to get this going again as quickly as possible. What do you think of that?'

'Well, let's look at that: the current round of tax cuts emanating from the election campaign is unlikely to be paid other than as cash, which means that we go into this post-boom phase of the stock market without a top-up to the 9 per cent which I left. Some in the higher echelons of the workforce will get to 12 and 15 per cent under their own steam because they are the ones who'll get investment advice, and some baby boomers will salary-sacrifice like there is no tomorrow to get as much money as they possible can in before they turn 65. But the great body of people will not get past 9 per cent as things stand. They won't salary-sacrifice: they don't have the money to salary-sacrifice, they don't have the advice to salary-sacrifice, and they don't have the incentive.

'So unless there is some wider plan by the government to get the bulk of employees up from 9 per cent to 12 and beyond that to 15, it won't happen. Even though if they last until 90 they are going to need hip replacements, their natural hips will wear out, they'll need some basic work on their hearts, their renal system may break down. So to keep a human being motoring until 90 is going to cost them more than 12 per cent of their working income in retirement. To take that savings proportion up for fundamental ageing reasons is now the first priority for when we resume what we began in the 1990s.

'When it is fiscally possible—when budget revenue returns to maintaining prudent levels to national income—some substantial proportion of revenue must go out as pension-fund saving, not as tax-cut cash. And we would be rash not to return to that, for such a variety of reasons, not just ageing reasons. Consider this: the difference between fiscal policy in Australia and fiscal policy in America, Britain, Germany, France—any other first world country you want to mention—is that in this country there is now another arm of policy available, another instrument of policy. And that is the ability to pay money into all these millions of super accounts. In those other countries, those millions of super accounts connected to the government do not exist. In Australia, any government now has the option of putting money into those accounts, whereas in the case of the American, or the German, or British treasury, there is not that option. You have a savings conduit constructed here by us in the 1990s which does not exist elsewhere in the OECD.'

Keating took a call on his mobile. For the first time, I was able to take a leisurely reconnaissance of the room in which we sat. On the right, against the wall, I studied another magnificent clock, this one in contrast with the ornate Louis XVIth which I had first noticed in front of me. The one on my right was from the period of the Directoire—say about 1800—the era of Napoleon and the new classicism. The figure of a woman beside the clock was clothed austerely. The stance was straight and severe; it was Ionic. And the style of the dress must have been the first display of the empire line, the waist immediately under the breasts, and the dress falling from there in a straight Grecian line. It was a style to be repeated in various modes and at various times in the centuries that followed. I wondered if, in its later appearances, there was some similar correlation between the style and the spirit of the times.

What struck me now was the unified theme in the room, of change, represented so dramatically in France, from a feudal landscape and social climate into the beginnings of the modern political landscape—a change reflected with rapidity in art, architecture, and decoration, and represented politically with the explosive power of the revolution and Napoleon.

I noted the change in Paul Keating from the frustrated man in the last years of the Howard government, ready to toss over to the unions the ambitions embodied in his pension framework with the cry that they should forget about government and go for what they could get from pensions by using their industrial power.

He hadn't really meant that. His creative ability had taken up the link between government budgets and the pension funds to the point where you could say a new theorem had emerged—a golden conduit. The pension funds would join the armoury of government instruments by allowing government, through the budget, to make co-payments into individual pensions in lieu of naked tax payments, according to whether total communal expenditure needed to be slowed or hastened. It was a brilliant concept and was, as he said, unique among developed economies.

Keating continued, 'I think by 2010 the government's solemn commitments on Howard's tax cuts will have been completed, which gives the Rudd government the option to reconsider the stance of fiscal policy. I think at that point prudence would say we ought to be able to grow compulsory super from 9 to 12 and in a subsequent move to 15.'

Our conversation moved to the contamination of Australian banks by their slide into borrowing US dollars as deposits. Keating made the point that Australia was an economy that grew by bringing money for investment from abroad, so that net borrowing from overseas had always been a basic part of our existence. But what mattered now was that investment borrowing was being joined at an accelerating pace by the spill abroad of borrowing to fund consumer spending, to the point where the country's net external debt was growing too fast. It was now the responsibility of government to budget for larger surpluses to offset some of this increased private-sector external borrowing.

He continued: 'Because we have been encouraging increased consumer spending through tax cuts without offsetting that with more savings through the budget—that is, higher budget surpluses—we are now putting an inordinate call on overseas debt which is having to be financed by short international securities of under a year raised by the four major banks. They are now borrowing their short-term deposits from overseas to an increasing extent.

'Borrowing in this international inter-bank market today, short-term—that is, under 12 months—is not something one would want to make a habit of. This is particularly so when you look at the overall international debt chart and see that our net foreign debt in total has grown from about $200 billion ten years ago to $600 billion today.

'You can see that the Howard government wanted the best of all worlds, and hang the consequences. They wanted the investment to keep us going at 4 per cent growth; they wanted the domestic spending, to be able to say they had unemployment continually falling; they wanted the terms-of-trade effect full-on us to keep our spending power rising; and they wanted the political benefits of tax cuts. The only measure of restraint on us was the Reserve Bank raising interest rates.

'In the end, you can't do all those things. Therefore, the spill on overseas funds which the Howard government's fiscal policy occasioned is something that we will now struggle with, because we have now got to fund these increasing obligations and find extra debt every month at enhanced international rates of interest.'

I asked Keating whether he thought the Australian banks would have been borrowing on the international market in this climate had his government remained in office.

Keating replied, 'With the long-running investment phase Australia has had, the answer is yes—but nothing like to this degree. What would have happened was that superannuation fund savings would have themselves gone up at least half a trillion dollars. In other words, the last 6 per cent added to the 9 per cent where we left would have been worth half a trillion. So that super, instead of being $1.1 trillion, would have been around $1.6 trillion. That would have funded a good deal more of the domestic investment here. With the extra take-off from booming terms of trade, we could have afforded by now 15 per cent super and budget surpluses much larger than we are running now. And that, by now, is what we should have had.

'This would have avoided the overheating and therefore the spill onto overseas funds. And it would have let investment pick up the trade account for us. What we got instead was a government which was just throwing the money around like there was no tomorrow. Of course, tomorrows do arrive. But the reason the Howard government was able to live like this was that it had no public debate. It had managed to stifle public debate—and, I must say, aided and abetted by the Treasury—in saying that the private current-account debt doesn't matter; it will get funded by the rest of the world ad infinitum. I've never believed that.'

David Love: 'And I might say, aided and abetted by the late Labor opposition.'

Paul Keating: 'Well, Kim Beazley, to give him his due, did speak about the current-account debt. When net international debt got over $500 billion he got into that. You see, when Costello and Howard first began pursuing me with the debt truck, our debt was $190 billion. Kim Beazley started drawing attention to it when it got over $500 billion. It's now a net $600 billion.'

'You see what Howard and Costello chose to campaign on in 1996 was the international debt of $190 billion. Then, when he becomes treasurer and begins to perceive what is happening under him, Costello drops all talk about the $190 billion and instead confines himself to taking about "the debt" and begins to talk about the debt of the Commonwealth. But when I left, Commonwealth debt to GDP was only 16 per cent anyway. About $10 billion. He really had a thimble-and-pea trick going. He followed the thimbles around the table: under which thimble is the figure of $190 billion and under which is the $10 billion Commonwealth debt?

'He talked about paying "the debt" off. And people believed that we'd paid the debt off. But we haven't paid "the debt" off at all. There's $600 billion of it sitting there, owing to foreigners. And at the wrong moment in history. We've got to keep funding it in the worst markets we've seen in 50 years.'

We turned to the international financial situation, and Keating observed that international financial crises in past decades had come from the developing world: the South American debt crisis in the 1980s, the Asian financial and economic crisis, the Russian debt crisis.

He continued: 'This time, the crisis is at the core of the Western financial system—the United States' financial system, and in its primary institutions. And it arose from the fact that as interest rates went down in the great softening under Greenspan, the capacity of people to refinance their mortgages from fixed rate to floating rate—where they previously might have had a fixed rate of 6, suddenly they're down to a floating rate of 1.5 per cent. They refinanced, and took the cash and spent it.

'A lot of them got into a situation where they didn't have the capacity to service their debt at something more like normal rates of interest. And financial institutions, being the Bourbons they are—they learn nothing and forget nothing—used this situation to burn up great chunks of their shareholders' capital. This time, however, their route is different. It's not developing-country debt they're burning up; this time, it's refinancing the housing debt of ordinary, middle-class Americans. This time, the problem is not liquidity, it is collateral. That collateral is the homes against which mortgages are held, and it has to be viewed as capital of the banks that is being destroyed. The banks are losing a large part of their shareholding base—their capital. And they're now having to go cap in hand to the Saudis, to other interests in the Middle East, to the Chinese, to the Singaporeans, to recapitalise the grandest of all American financial institutions. Now this tells you something about prudential policy in the United States, and it goes back to the whole question of banks: banks in the end are nothing but franchises of the central bank, and when push comes to shove they rely on the central bank to be the lender of the first resort.'

'The last resort?'

'No, the first resort. Because the banks have become frightened to lend to one another, the only lenders now are the central banks. And if central banks are lenders of the first resort, how can we put up with chief executive officers of banks paying themselves $15 or $20 million a year when they know that, when the old question of moral hazard arises, the central banks will bail out their franchisees?

'So the problem now has become the philosophy underlying the banking system. We need a review of the prudential code about how these banks conduct themselves. But we don't seem to be going to get that because every time an unforeseen problem arises, the banks go into the central bank and make money by exploiting the weakness that has arisen.

'This is what they did with the sub-prime crisis, and as a result we have a much wider crisis. Until the remuneration structure of banks has changed to one where they are given salaries and share options on the basis of performance over a much longer period, say, five to ten years—so that we know that the tenure of a particular group hasn't shot the bank's capital—then the group shouldn't be rewarded as it is now. Until there is a genuine guide as to what has been the contribution of a particular group to the capital of the business and its earnings growth, they shouldn't be paid the options to cash in on the stock exchange. If short-termism and opportunism leads to big chunks of capital being lost, you are asking for trouble to pay the options. It is the present philosophy that lies behind the financial crisis now being faced.

'The banks know that if a particular bet goes bad their institution won't fail, because the central banks will bail them out; the biggest central bank, the American Fed, will again relax interest rates. So we have to know now that when you see bank chiefs stand up they are not the leonine figures of the financial system but, rather, bureaucrats who happen to be lucky enough to have inherited a particular franchise at a particular time.'

From the decline in attention to moral hazard in the banking system, we moved to financial innovation which, Paul Keating observed, had allowed the financial-services sector of the world economy to grow very large: 'This means that we are now hostage to the financial component of the economy more than we ever were before, to the point where the problems of the financial economy are beyond reach and remedy of the central banks.

'All that central banks do now is hope and pray that they get big, positive market effects from the little changes they make in softening credit and so on. But in terms of going to the source of the problem and dealing with the massive level of derivatives out there, or the massive growth of other derived forms of finance, the central banks are not in a position to do this.

'So the world economy has now become hostage to the first world financial system—not the third world anymore. And this is going to be a very trying time for governments and regulators. And a dangerous time for us to be as exposed as we are.'

We moved in focus from the international sweep to the domestic institutions that had grown up out of his watch and to the pressure they were now taking from the hedge funds. I mentioned Macquarie Group.

Paul Keating: 'Macquarie Group is a classic example of an

institution in a very open financial economy able to do new things and develop new products. Now, there's an on-balance set of judgements here: is the world better off with fungible capital markets across borders and financial innovations of the kind Macquarie has helped create. I say, yes, we are better off. But does it mean that we are going to have a trouble-free time when aggregates get out of line? To some extent it is out of our hands. It comes down to how careful and skilful the international central banks can be. Central banks have got to be very wary about what is now called the Greenspan put—that is, that central banks are not only expected but obliged to soften monetary conditions regardless of economic needs, so as to bail out managers of financial institutions who have over-bent themselves. This is going to take some working through, and we are only part way through it now.

'Now, let me say that I don't think the Australian institutions are as vulnerable as others because mainly their initiatives have been well collateralised—there's no fashion for sub-prime lending here by our institutions. But we will yet wait and see whether the "fees model" is going to work; that is where a financial institution develops a series of assets, mainly infrastructure assets, on their balance sheet, takes them off their balance sheet, puts them into a fund, sells that fund on the market, and then takes a fee for operating the business and that fund—'

David Love: 'That is the Macquarie model.'

Paul Keating: 'Well, yes. The question is, what is the lot of those unit-holders who own the units in these unit trusts, which hold the title to these infrastructure assets, which are operated by the investment banks taking fees? Well, you have to say that a lot of the assets are underperforming. And you have to know that the ability of the financial institutions to keep digging up new sources of fees by tipping good assets into underperforming funds may stop. But that is an altogether different problem to the kind we have in the United States; what we have there is a packet of bonds which reflect maybe a billion dollars worth of mortgages, of which a number of slices of those bonds are worthless. They're not simply underperforming, they just don't perform. And it is the problem that these people have brought to the central financial market of the world, New York, in which all of our institutions participate and borrow, and this is projecting the problem on to us rather than any specific problems generated here.'

David Love: 'This climate emanating from New York has given the hedge funds a new lease of life. They're ready to have a go at anything. How vulnerable are we to them? We know how rapacious they can be, given the Thai experience et al. in your day.'

Paul Keating: 'Well, this sort of market suits the hedge fund. They make money on the way up and the way down. A hedge fund in the last few weeks, for instance, could have been buying Centro Property shares at one price, betting that the price of those shares will keep falling so that they can give the purchaser of the shares from them shares that the hedge fund bought at a lower price. Now is that kind of scavenging always unhealthy? I tend to think it isn't, providing that the financial aggregates are right.

'The hedge funds can hasten corrections that may have to be made. I do come back to the point that the basic problems came from an excess of liquidity stemming from monetary policies which were too soft in the United States, and in such a situation the scavengers can thrive. No amount of slicing and dicing into various packages can turn a bad credit into a good credit. If the underlying assets are good, the credits reflecting them will be okay; but when a bad credit is sliced and diced away into a whole lot of instruments whose apparent value cannot be easily discerned, then we're in the path way to trouble, and the hedge fund probably has a role in cleaning it up.

'Experience by finance institutions, prudential management, hopefully, will sharpen our noses for the more dangerous excesses in financial engineering—that is, financial engineering which simply seeks to hide the underlying inadequacy of assets in order to take a fee on the way through.'

David Love: 'So we may have a scary period while we sort the good residual from the bad in these sliced and diced packages?'

Paul Keating: 'I think so. There is still the prevalent notion that central banks can throw a switch and everything will be alright. But this problem is now so big—the growth in fungible financial assets has been so profound—that it has gone beyond the remedy of central banks. That's the great worry. All you can hope now is that people in the market take the signals that are now being given out by central banks and act better accordingly. Because central banks won't have the financial wherewithal, the mechanical wherewithal, to actually change things themselves.'

David Love: 'In preparing this book, something that particularly strikes me is that about 60,000 young Australians apply for jobs at Macquarie Group each year, of which they take, maybe, 300. It seems that we are now a people forever voyaging in quest of a greater part to play in the world, like the Venetians. What is going to happen to the aspirations of our clever young?'

Paul Keating: 'I think Australian financial innovation has led the world. Not only Macquarie Group and Babcock & Brown. You see it in property in companies like Westfield, in real estate investment trusts, in cross-border leasing; you can see it in many things. All that's good: the growth now in Macquarie and Babcock & Brown is much greater abroad than it is in Australia. There's a big tick here for financial innovation.

'What we don't want is too much crying when the party's ended. There is a case now for the regulators being quite hard, to keep all the arteries open. The Australian Bankers' Association has been going on now for years about getting rid of the four pillars policy, their object being to let the four banks merge into two. That's not what we want. The thing that will stick to a society like ours, particular in times of a financial crunch, is diversity of ownership, so that one balance sheet is not contaminated with the other. We certainly don't want to promote contagion by taking two eggs and making an omelette, by having a diminution of competition.'

David Love: 'Isn't one of our constraining problems that there is this one licensed investment bank, Macquarie Group, that stands out and attracts the scavengers, as you call them. And if we are going to properly exploit the resource of 60,000 young people anxious to go on this world-wide voyage from Australia, we are going to need more and more domestic capital, turbo-charging more and more ships.'

Paul Keating: 'Well we've got two such investment banks now, with Babcock. But it's not just a matter of financial capital; we need intellectual capital through education. And it's not just a matter of mass output; it's quality. The pool of superannuation assets is going to bring forward a host of managers. All sorts of people are going to be packaging Australian financial resources into investable asset classes. Certainly, we don't want this only done by one or two institutions.'

David Love: 'If things had turned out differently and you had been able to move more swiftly to your 15 per cent, so that what you have called the turbo-charging of the markets could have proceeded at a greater pace, where would we have been by now in this voyaging?'

Paul Keating: 'Well, let's say, with all conservatism, we would have been at least $400 billion in front; probably closer to $500 billion. That's if we had done the 3 per cent in 1997–98 when I legislated for it. Given that our net foreign debt abroad is $600 billion, we would, for one thing, have had a big proportion of that covered by extra domestic assets, and we would have been freer to move domestically and internationally. The quicker we get back to structured savings through such things as the pension funds, the better. That's one thing.

'Secondly, we can't just see the super funds as troughs for Macquarie, or Babcock & Brown, or any of the others, to scoop up funds and put them off into specialised vehicles charging big fees. That cannot go on; certainly not at the fees being charged. And I don't think private equity is going to be able to go on doing what it's been doing, either — taking huge fees on the way through. The cheap debt that kept this going is itself gone. So what we need is a plethora of managers all engaged in competition in this asset pool of ours. This, in itself, will mean that there is greater protection for what we've got going, and higher earnings for those superannuants who have trusted their incomes and their savings to these institutions.'

David Love: 'If your original schema finally gets into place, do we have lots of new institutional units employing the 60,000?'

Paul Keating: 'Yes. This is a massive new industry. Superannuation savings is a massive new industry. Funds management in Australia is a massive new industry …'

'But what about financial products?'

'What we need for that is more competition in the industry. More competition will mean lower fees and less risk and more products. As the system grows in scale and size, fees for management drop, and there is less risk occasioned by having too much of it in one or two baskets. And from that we will be bigger and bigger as a financial force because the savings pool will be growing at a rapid rate; and as long as we have the managers to manage it, we become more and significant in the world. The Australian superannuation savings pool is now fourth in the world; by next year, it will be number three; in not too many years, it will become number two.

'With such a massive pool of savings, even at 9 per cent we would go to something like three trillion dollars. With movement to 12 and then to 15, of course the whole thing will accelerate. With a vat of funds that large, you will find the institutions coming here. Of course, we won't be able to invest this all in Australia—the vat will be too large—they'll have to be invested abroad, which will take us into Asia generally, China, North America, Eastern Europe …'

David Love: 'It seems quite phenomenal. This little place that grew up on hacking and tilling away at drought-struck soil promises to become such a financial-services power.'

Paul Keating: 'I think we already are. The phenomenal thing is the chance to grow at a great clip. You will see institutions both coming up and coming in. People like Vanguard, the great American investment-management company, are coming in and saying, 'We will take a bet for you on your stock market but, instead of charging you 1 per cent, we'll charge you 0.3'. That is, you'll get the same service for a third the price from a major international institution. So you see these major institutions moving in competitively. They are doing this because this is one of the great vats of change around the world.'

We ended our conversation, and Paul inquired about me getting back to central Sydney. I said I would walk up to the Cross for old times' sake, to the tube station. In a delightful reversion to the other Keating, after all that depth and clarity, he said: 'You'd better be careful some young sheila doesn't jump you up there, mate.'

I replied that, like the Australian economy at this point in early 2008, I would take my chances.

Chapter 13

Completing The Revolution

'There are more things in heaven and earth, Horatio,
Than are dreamt of in your philosophy'.
–*Hamlet,* William Shakespeare

IN THE MIDDLE DECADES OF THE TWENTIETH CENTURY, A new genre of American literature, the Southern Gothic movement, bloomed. This writing was drawn from people and places of the old South. It was not preoccupied with the Confederacy; it marked itself out by the singular sensibility of Southern towns and populations sixty to a hundred years on from the Civil War. A stock part of Southern Gothic literature has been the plight of those ostracised by traditional Southern culture, such as the heroines of Tennessee Williams' plays like Blanche DuBois in *A Street Car Named Desire*, the disturbed loner of a Southern dynasty in *Cat on a Hot Tin Roof,* the forms of madness in a Southern town represented by William Faulkner.

Harper Lee, the author of *To Kill a Mockingbird,* provides a real-life picture of Southern Gothic at work in her reminiscences of growing up in Monroeville, Alabama. A close friend of her childhood in the town was Truman Capote, who came to town every summer and lived with his aunts next door to Harper Lee. Capote was ridiculed in the town because he was different; for one thing, he could not help displaying his advanced vocabulary.

On a broader, more complex, scale there is something of the same Southern Gothic attribute in Australia's continuing attitude to Paul Keating: the antipathy towards one who dares to be truculently different. It is alright so long as he presents himself as the figure of fun a la *Keating!,* the musical. But let him parade himself as a financial mentor for Australia, and there are many people who can't cope with such an idea. He is on the advisory board of the Development Bank of China, and he talks to the European Union on pension policy: top European officials would give their eye teeth to have the kind of pensions policy for workers that he initiated here. But no official institution in Australia seeks his counsel. The citizens of Monroeville, Alabama eschewed the advanced vocabulary of Truman Capote.

Earlier in 2008 (on 23 February), I read a commentary piece from *Sydney Morning Herald* columnist Annette Sampson on the idea of putting some of the promised tax cuts through into superannuation. 'That reeks of the Keating era,' she said. That jarred with me a little and sent me reaching for a dictionary. There are a couple of definitions of 'reek': one is of something that smokes, steams, or fumes; the other is of 'a distinctive odour that is offensively unpleasant.' The immediate impact of the word in Sampson's context is a mixture of both definitions, with sufficient of the latter to remind me of the Southern Gothic. It strikes the chord in defining how negatively Keating is still regarded by a surprising number of Australians. The Howard government encouraged this reaction, of course, and one can dismiss that as party politics. But one cannot so easily dismiss the negativity from much of his own party that is still aimed towards Keating. In this, there is more of Monroeville's reaction to Truman Capote.

One should say this: we have looked far enough and long enough into the extraordinary malaise infecting the international economy from its American credit base to say that the Rudd government needs a sharper response than it presently evokes. The best start it can make is a change in attitude, practically and symbolically, towards Paul Keating and his works. A more hard-edged strategy and philosophy is what the Keating revolution offers. There is already a perceivable danger that, before the government's first term is through, the asset wealth of middle Australia will be diminishing. The world's stock markets will rebound and retract in a slow dance with the world's central banks and their ever-more-ingenious manipulations designed to put a floor under the markets. But the underlying asset structure of the United States will not be fixed so easily. Australia, will have to live with what goes on in the belly of America. The most promising proposal for dealing with this malaise is Keating's golden-conduit idea, which was sketched in the previous chapter.

There are two lines of reasoning for saying this. First, the international one: despite huge efforts and rapid moves in recent months by the US and other international central banks to ease pressure on credit in the international system, there are hard-heads on Wall Street who do not believe they have dealt with the problem. Their scepticism is based on the deduction that the US Federal Reserve has greatly underestimated the problem of lurking debt beyond that festering in the sub-prime mortgage regions of the States.

What the Fed doesn't—perhaps can't—take sufficient account of is the huge proliferation of unexposed financial risk involved in the growth of the derivatives business. According to figures collated at the world's clearinghouse for financial information, the Bank for International Settlements, at Basle in Switzerland, the quantum of derivatives trade presently at large in the world is $516 trillion, an almost unimaginable figure and a five-fold increase in five years. To get some idea of the enormity of this, note that the current total of US money supply outstanding is $15 trillion.

In this setting, one must expect the medium-term outlook to be one of fits and starts, of market rises and falls. Internationally, a market plunge and an interest-rate jerk upwards will be met by world central bank action led by the US Fed, and the market will come back up again for a while. But with such out-of-control debt exposure lurking, no government can expect early peace of mind. From cyberspace, which is where many of the most complex debt derivatives whirl around, could come sudden debt crises affecting the credit base of the banks. These derivative-based crises will be similar to the sub-prime mortgages crisis, which was derived not so much from the mortgages themselves but rather from the discovery that they had been sliced and diced into seemingly kosher securities bought and sold in markets far beyond the ken of home buyers in Michigan, California, and Florida. And for reasons already sketched through this book, Australia is at the leading edge of world exposure to complex credit derivatives. Australia's exposure was adequately demonstrated in the autumn of 2008 when the banking sector of the market, the diadem, fell 35 per cent below the level it had been in late 2007, in the space of three months.

The other line of reasoning is domestic: the extent to which the Australian household sector has allowed itself to become highly leveraged to debt. Morgan Stanley Research reports that the Australian household-debt relationship to household income is almost 200 per cent. This mattered relatively little while Australian household-asset prices—largely, the price of one's home—rose. Seeing home prices rise relative to the mortgages raised to buy those homes has become a way of life in Australia, and this has been a major factor in accelerating national spending relative to national saving—a proclivity which made the Australian financial system so heavily dependent on international markets for funding.

It did not matter much in relative terms while the rest of the world saw Australia and China bound together in response to a joyous surge in demand for Australian resources and thus a surge in prices for Australian commodities. In this situation, the rest of the world was quite happy to have Australian debt—that is, to put money into Australian bank deposits. Compared to what the rest of world paid for international short-term debt, we were getting it cheaply.

Signs that Australia's blighted access to relatively cheap international short-term debt (in the form of bank deposits) may not be just a factor of the US credit mess are flashing from Chinese inflation figures. In assessing Chinese inflation, one must allow something for the distortions that a savage winter forced on food supply. But, even allowing for that, Chinese inflation is on an ominously rising trend: the country's inflation accelerated from its usual level of 2 per cent at the beginning of 2007 to an 8 per cent rate in early 2008.

What does this have to do with the interest rates for Australian banks? It means that China, like it or not, is going to have to change its managed exchange-rate so that there is greater consideration given to Chinese consumers relative to industrial investors. China is going to have to let in cheaper food. For the dictatorship to ignore the warning signs of the past year would be to risk social unrest at a more than usually dangerous time for them. To swing policy in favour of the Chinese consumer, China is going to have to allow the Chinese currency, per unit, to be worth more and more, so that it becomes cheaper for its people to buy consumer goods from the rest of the world. It is going to have to let the yuan strengthen more and more relative to the US dollar, and accept that it won't sell its products so easily to export markets. Ultimately, this amounts to a swing against Australian resource exports and, ultimately, against Australia's terms of trade and against the Australian dollar and its concomitant international interest-rate cost. This is not going to happen overnight, but we must have policies that prepare for it.

The policies we have had in place for a number of years now are the antithesis of what we should have had: domestic savings are down relative to domestic spending, and the result is that banks are scrambling to raise funds from a diminished pool of deposits. This results, in turn, in upward pressure on basic bank interest-rate costs above the level set by the Reserve Bank. At the same time, the banks have to meet increased local demand for longer-term money as Australian businesses lose their direct access to international bond markets. For this, the banks have no alternative but to go abroad and pay a going higher rate.

Look around you at the warning signs: the Australian current account deficit reached 7 per cent of gross national product in the first half of 2008, and the details of the balance-of-payments figures show that this is now largely the result of a need to increase the application of funds to servicing our foreign debt. This means that, despite the incredible surge in the prices of Australia's internationally sold commodities, Australia's underlying external-account balance is weakening. Despite the huge current strength in our resource industries, foreign willingness to take up Australian short-term debt (bank deposits) without a greater interest-rate reward is weakening. The international dollar market has begun to seek a discount for Australian bank deposits and, with the Australian household debt-to-income ratio at 200 per cent, each rise of 1 per cent in the bank interest rate will lift the debt burden on households by 2 per cent. In 2009 we are at risk of stagflation: cost pressure on prices and interest rates at a time of declining economic activity.

So what does a Labor government do? Its path has been made more difficult by the party having abandoned the Keating strategy after the coalition's election win in 1996. I have explained how this—along with the coalition overspending domestically—has created a long-run swing towards insufficient domestic saving relative to spending, and how this has in turn exposed our banking system to the problems of the collapse of the US credit system in 2007. This, in turn, produced a sudden slump in the market prices of our banking shares, and hence a sudden slump in the reported values of our pension funds' portfolios.

The Rudd government's unfortunate nominee for dealing with this problem was Senator Nick Sherry, who revealed once again his lack of comprehension of the economic relevance of Keatings' drive towards a 15 per cent pension regime. He did more than that: in public comments, he unnecessarily injected fear into the superannuation community. The performance of Senator Sherry, both in his long-run incomprehension of what Keating was about and his inadequate handling of public relations on the recent superannuation slump, has robbed Labor of what should have been a telling defence and an advantageous point of attack: that the coalition had cut off at the knees the Keating construction of a balance between domestic spending and domestic saving by refusing to sustain his drive towards a 15 per cent industrial ratio by 2000. 'Now look at the result', Labor could have said. 'If the original Keating target had been sustained, there would have been no sudden banking-share slump in 2008 and no pensioner disillusionment.'

There is, now, the understandable fear of pensioners about putting more money into superannuation funds. In addition, the government can't explain why the slump in the value of pensioners' holdings was the result of the country not having saved enough relative to our spending, and can't articulate how the original destruction of superannuation policy contributed to this. The Rudd government must find within itself a capacity for a coherent explanation, in terms that bewildered pensioners can understand, of why an advance in the industrial pension ratio is a vital part of the solution. It must organise a move as fast as it can towards shifting tax cuts from the existing current account-expanding approach to a delayed-spending approach in the form of contributions on behalf of taxpayers to industrial pension funds.

The answer to this is the Keating conduit scheme that has been made possible by his 1990s policy actions. But the appearance of Nick Sherry as a frightener in the autumn of 2008 raises questions about the Rudd government's capacity, comprehension, and will to handle the necessary advance of the revolution. It must first show a readiness to remove Senator

Sherry, and the left-wing conservatism he represents, from this complex task with its wide-ranging implications. Nick Sherry is its declared enemy, and his appearance in March 2008 as the spokesman for pensions policy does not instil any confidence that Labor will take enough action. Rapid application of the Keating conduit is by far the most effective way of getting household savings to grow strongly relative to household outlays: in financial terms, this would boost the supply of domestic bank deposits relative to international ones, with figures in the area of $500 billion extra potentially available.

This would not only cut exposure to tainted US dollars; it would also change the balance of supply relative to demand in domestic deposits, which would then lower their interest price. This is the escape route from the crazy level of exposure that the country now has to a proportion of the US$516 trillion in debt derivatives that are floating around, which currently has the potential to be disastrous for Australia. The Rudd government has inherited this situation from the Howard–Costello government, but a successful exculpation and advance requires greater nous and organisation than the Rudd government has thus far displayed.

I MUST NOW GO FURTHER into the maze of the polluted international markets. The sub-prime mortgage crisis arose because loose US monetary policy encouraged mortgage-brokers, financed by banks, to talk people who couldn't afford it into taking out mortgages to buy homes. More and more of these mortgage-takers defaulted, some mortgage-brokers went broke, and the banks that had financed them lost capital. If that had been all, the US would have had a nasty regional financial setback, and there it would have stopped.

But it didn't stop there, and there are several reasons why. The first is that modern financial engineers are no longer content to have a batch of mortgages in the bank's safe. Instead, the mortgages can be gathered together and 'securitised'; that is, they are gathered in sufficient numbers, insured, and introduced to the world as a new security big enough for major pension funds, life offices, and the like to treat as a portfolio asset. The principle is the same one I traced when tracking the evolution of Hill Samuel Australia into Macquarie Group: in the 1970s, Hill Samuel started the process of collecting mortgages in sufficient bundles, insuring them with the Commonwealth's Home Loans Insurance Corporation, and selling them to asset-starved life offices and pension funds.

But there the similarity ends: the Australian packages were homogenous, high-quality mortgages insured by a sufficiently impregnable government entity to allow the resulting packages to be blue-chip securities. In the American case, the financial engineers decided to include some sub-prime mortgages in the bundles of new securities, which they called MBSs (mortgage-backed securities). The appeal of having some 'sub-primes' in the package was that the sub-primes, being risky loans, carried high interest rates. These mortgage-backed securities nonetheless became bonds in the sense of a Commonwealth bond or an electricity company bond that you buy from your broker or bank, and they were bought and sold widely across the world's financial markets.

The sub-prime mortgage crisis moved from being a segmented regional disaster, to a national disaster, and then an international disaster, when slices of sub-prime mortgages within the widely disseminating mortgage-backed securities began to become the victims of old-fashioned family disasters. As the US housing market sank, more and more families had to walk away from their mortgages; the calamity of the family hearth became a calamity on Wall Street because big banks, pension funds, managed funds, and the like suddenly found themselves in a crisis of confusion. Could the collapsing sub-prime component of their bonds somehow be separated from the non-sub-prime segments? Were the capital losses in bond prices limited to sub-prime losses? Were the sub-prime, tainted mortgage-backed securities worth anything? The answer to each of these questions was no.

This calamity began to impact on Australian finance via its reliance on US dollar deposits, in part through fear. Because banks and others at the world's centre of finance could not say where and when these explosive mortgage-backed securities were likely to turn up in their asset base, even the biggest names in US banking became wary of one another. The old easy flow of deposits—borrowing from one bank to another—began to seize up. It might seem unthinkable, but even the most supposedly secure financial houses could open their mortgage-backed securities bundle and find bankruptcy and default exploding in their faces.

So the flow of funds from one bank to another began to cease, and an involuntary, unofficial credit squeeze began. George W. Bush's tax cuts had no bearing on this situation, although he didn't seem to grasp why this should be so. Words of reassurance from Ben Bernanke, the chairman of the Federal Reserve, had insufficient effect. The now randomly explosive sub-prime mortgage collapse got worse, and the banks' attitude to one another deteriorated from wariness to open mistrust, with each charging the other higher interest rates for lending base-rate money. In Australia, we began to see this take shape as our own banks started to add extra interest-rate charges onto the policy-based rises of the Reserve Bank.

The extraordinary reverberations of the sub-prime mortgage affair are not through yet. Thus far, analysis of the fall-out has been confined to that area of American and international finance still under the direction of the world's central banks. Its potential for damage goes further when we move into the most recent product of world financial engineering—the derivatives market. Here, we part company from any semblance of sovereign government. We confront that almost inconceivable figure of trading value compiled by the Bank for International Settlements which, in recent years, has rocketed upwards—the $516 trillion derivatives-market debt mentioned earlier.

As US and other banks tried to cover their risks from mortgage-backed securities, they moved into these ungoverned financial derivatives. Here, they could take a position to protect themselves from further mortgage-backed securities implosions. The most basic way to do this was to buy what is known as a plain vanilla swap—which is when the market risk of loss from one asset can be swapped, at a price, for a stream of income from another asset. Once the swap is done, a new derivative is formed which then takes on a life of its own and can be metastasised into all sorts of varieties of derivatives beyond the plain vanilla, and which eventually require a mathematician to understand.

The varieties of swaps out there involving the original sub-prime mortgages would presumably be a fraction of the $516 trillion total. But it is not the quantity that matters in this fantastic scenario. It is the tension and stupor created in what should be a fluid world financial system. There is now a fear of the unknown: that out there, somewhere, is an entity which, without warning, could reveal a collapsed sub-prime slice which could suddenly implode, leaving its holder with fresh losses. The possibilities of losses in the derivatives market reinforces the reluctance of financial institutions to do business with one another except on the basis of stricter limitations and higher interest rates.

This scenario is just one strand of the sub-prime crisis. There is another strand, insurance, running in parallel, which must also concern investors. You will recall that when Hill Samuel Australia was setting up its particular mortgage-backed securities back in the 1970s, an essential part of making the mortgage bundle a gilt-edged security was the insuring of it with the Commonwealth's Home Loans Insurance Corporation. The idea of a home loans guarantee institution in Australia came from the United States. The Australian entity, however, is a cleaner concept than the semi-detached operations in the States. The principal players among these US insurance entities are the Federal National Mortgage Association (Fannie Mae) and the Federal Home Mortgage Corporation (Freddie Mac). We are yet to see the reports of the full impact of the crisis upon these two entities.

But there is more than enough to digest from two speciality American insurers called Municipal Bond Investment Assurance (MBIA) and American Municipal Bond Assurance Corporation (Ambac)—different from Fannie Mae and Freddie Mac, in that Fannie and Freddie were always in the business of directly insuring American mortgages, while MBIA and Ambac were, until recently, keeping to the business of insuring bonds, unrelated to housing, and issued by perfectly respectable US municipalities. They were known as monoline insurers. Recently, however, these two municipal specialists became discontented with insuring municipal bonds alone and got into the business of insuring the bundles of mortgage-backed home loan securities (MBS), with their fatal ingredient of sub-prime mortgages.

The Wall Street traders had to have this blue chip insurance to give their MBS bundles the quality they needed—supposedly top-line investment status, allowing them to be freely traded. Unfortunately the two venerable insurers of municipal bonds had years of status, but they didn't have federal government ownership. For generations, it didn't seem to matter. They were the institutions that supported municipal government, insuring the payment of principal and interest on municipal bonds. They had credit ratings of AAA, and the bonds they insured were thus rated AAA. That they should take on the job of insuring the securities which Wall Street had created from a mixture of prime and sub-prime mortgage bundles seemed like a good idea at the time. And they were attracted by the higher fees available.

It turned out, though, that the bond insurers had no idea just how risky these new-fangled packages were. They gravely underestimated how likely it was that the mortgage loans would go bad, which meant that they didn't charge enough for the guarantees they were offering. Their potential losses have turned into tens of billions of dollars, and estimates are that they'll need more than $100 billion to restore themselves to health. But the implications here, no less than in the case of inter-bank relations, go far beyond the direct losses suffered by the institutions.

Once a municipal-standard bond was given full guarantee by its insurance corporation, the bonds automatically got a

AAA rating from the American credit-rating agencies, such as Moody's and Standard and Poor's. This AAA rating gave them effortless trading status in the great markets of the world. And, like the MBS, in the hands of the banks they were turned into derivatives, free to float off in various forms into the stratosphere.

Among the biggest customers of municipal bond insurers have been the American pension funds, who would take anything the bond insurers had to offer at a AAA rating. Indeed, for interest-bearing securities outside governments, the pension funds were more or less confined to the products of the monolines because the trust deeds of the pension funds prohibited them from taking anything less than AAA ratings. But now, the startling losses that have been suffered by the insurers on the sliced and diced mortgage-backed securities bonds are forcing the credit agencies to reconsider their AAA ratings for the monoline insurance companies because they don't have government ownership. In fact, one of these insurers was downgraded to AA, and at the time of writing was desperately seeking additional capital to regain its AAA rating. For a monoline insurer, being downgraded from AAA to AA is a dreadful result. Worse than that, a loss of its AAA rating would mean that American pension funds are holding securities that they are prohibited from owning.

This may sound somewhat arcane, but its implications are potentially widespread. If the American pension funds decide they must sell their mortgage-backed securities at a loss, or indeed any securities from a monoline insurer whose AAA rating is under threat, the flow-on effects could cascade around the world, affecting the capital transactions of countries and companies that have never heard of the American specialist institutions involved. The same stultifying uncertainties that hit the banks would apply, extending into the never-never land of derivatives. Capital activity could effectively ice over—and the freeze could reach Australia, which imports much of its investment capital, and is poorly placed on its external account to withstand the shock from this.

In all this, there is a great urgency pressing upon Australia to go through a period of adjusting its national outlays to total savings. The Keating creed, with its conduits into the Australian pension funds, throws a lifeline to the Rudd government that it will belittle at its peril.

FINALLY, WE SHOULD CONSIDER the Japanese syndrome. After a huge property and share-market boom in the 1980s, the Japanese central bank took strong tightening action in the late 1980s—and got more than it bargained for. The boom was already overblown when central bank action began in earnest, and after 1990 the boom resoundingly collapsed. After decades of miracle-economy growth, the Japanese miracle faded completely. Japan has never adequately recovered; after a long period of post-boom stagnation, it slipped from recession into what can only be called a depression for a period around the turn of the century. The great post-war juggernaut became a memory, and among the cognoscenti 'Japan passing' became a somewhat sneering catchphrase. The phrase was meant to imply that Japan was not only being passed in a fast-changing world, but indeed that the place could no longer be taken seriously.

From about 2002, Japan began to grow again, though not rapidly. It seemed at least that the nightmare period was over. But by 2007 the slump had set in again. The stock market was once more falling alarmingly. The particular relevance of all this to my tale is that there is now a view in the United States that the Japanese pattern could be what lies in store for America.

No one perceives a parallel in the origins: there is no extraordinary 1980s Japan-style bubble to look back on in the US, and there was not the same slashing of interest rates that produced the Japanese bubble nor the leap in official interest rates which broke it. But what worries some observers of Japan and the United States is that there is a whiff of the early 1990s' post-bubble behaviour in Japan to be seen now in the US. On a less drastic scale, there is a fair array of post-1990 Japan detritus now hanging around in the US. As a result of the late 1980s credit crunch coming too late in the bubble, Japan suffered a stock-market crash probably only exceeded by Wall Street in 1929. Conventional wisdom says—or at least used to say—that when stocks fall, you move into real estate, which the Japanese did energetically. But in the Japanese case, this counter-balancing in investment strategy proved disastrous. What we can now recognise, retrospectively, as a variation of the US sub-prime phenomenon began to take hold, although at higher levels of the social strata. As an index of the health of land and real estate prices, the Japanese use—or used to use—the price of membership in top-line golf clubs. This index shows very neatly just how little use it was to diversify into real estate during the Japanese crunch: between late 1990 and late 1992, the price index for Tokyo Golf Club membership fell by about 70 per cent.

Behind this apparent picture of the travail of the wealthy that was provided by the plunge in the club's membership price lay a more mundane reality: bankruptcies on land, residences, condominiums, and businesses proliferated. Here is where the element of similarity between Japan and the US provokes the attention of the more pessimistic of international observers. In the hope that something would turn up, the Japanese banks held the sour mortgage loans on their books for years, stultifying the banks' own abilities to strike out afresh. The Japanese central bank encouraged them to carry these loans, pouring out credit to support real estate collateral worth perhaps 60 per cent of its value when the loans were made.

The central bank made no objection when the banks used the cheap credit pushed on them to increase their liquidity rather than to expand their lending. At the same time, the Japanese government was pursuing a George W. Bush-type course of cutting taxes and raising spending. Between 1992 and 1995, the Japanese government tried six such fiscal packages, to no avail. The benighted property-holders and business-owners sat frozen in fear and confusion as their banks carried them through, clinging to the hope that the next year would be better and they could get going again, and in the meantime taking no notice of the fiscal stimuli being thrust upon them by the central government. Here is where, by 2008, the more cynical minds in the US had begun to spot a paradigm. While not enough time has passed to test the paradigm, elements of it have appeared over recent months.

There are some Japanese-paradigm checkpoints you can watch for as the situation unfolds in America. The great Japanese collapse provided a battleground for the two principal canons of economics as it is practised in Japan and America—that is, Keynesian and monetarism. Japan provided a vast field for dissection and dispute about why neither monetarism nor Keynesianism worked.

For the monetarists, calls for action seemed to be adequately satisfied by a big expansion of the Japanese money base. This was demonstrated by enough money going into the system to drive down the bank rate from 6 per cent in 1990 to 4.5 per cent in 1991, 3.25 per cent in 1992, 1.75 per cent in 1993–94, and 0.5 per cent during 1995–2000. None of it did any good, and the monetarists' explanation for its failure is that in the preceding deflationary action the Bank of Japan had cut monetary expansion too quickly. Instead of using the money that the central bank was injecting, the fearful Japanese banks simply increased their liquidity base. Monetary policy couldn't work, the monetarists said, because the central bank let what is known as a liquidity trap develop.

For the Keynesians, Japan had seemed a perfect setting for their policy prescriptions to work. Aggregate demand had collapsed because investment had collapsed; using a favourite phrase of Keynes, 'animal spirits' had collapsed in the business sector. So the thing for central government to do was to take the place of business investment by raising its own spending to restore the level of aggregate demand. Between 1992 and 1995, the Japanese government launched six successive spending programmes, totalling 65.5 trillion yen, while at the same time cutting tax rates. In April 1998, the government came up with another fiscal-stimulus package of 16.7 trillion yen, then followed that through in November with a package worth 23.9 trillion yen. A year later came another fiscal package of 18 trillion yen, and then in October 2000 another package of 11 trillion yen. Overall, through the 1990s, Japan tried fiscal packages amounting to more than 100 trillion yen, causing 'on budget' public debt to exceed 100 per cent of Japan's GDP. None of it worked. The Keynesian explanation for the failure was that the Japanese government had failed to use fiscal policy well. It kept stopping and starting.

In the same way as the Russian revolutionaries of 1917 had their eyes constantly on the French revolutionaries of 1789, the front-line generals and observers of the American crisis have had their eye constantly on the Japanese debacle. They are, they say, determined not to make the same mistakes. With this resolution in place, the relevant US authorities have faced the world with all the appropriate declarations of determination to bring this debt-based American disaster to a swift and clean conclusion. Keynesian weapons in the form of presidential action to cut taxes and expand spending, as well as monetarist weapons in the form of central bank action to flood the system with money, have been brought into play. The difference between this restorative action and the terrible Japanese example, we were assured, would be the absence of hesitation, countering distress wherever it occurred, and expediting a quick correction of any further decline wherever it was perceived.

So the year 2008 began with a strong hope that the so-called American 'sub-prime mortgage crisis' would soon be a passing memory and that the housing markets and share portfolios of millions and millions of careful householders across the world would soon be back to where they were. Brokers perceived factors that would crystallise into a resurgence. Signals pointed towards taking advantage of this slump—to get back in there and buy—and people acted upon them in the first half of 2008. But, as the year progressed, there emerged from Washington and New York indications that, despite the flurry of action at the Fed and the Oval Office, and despite the enormous amount of federal money flooding into the market, the system was not firing as well as hoped.

The case of Bear Sterns illustrates the failure of the American efforts to demonstrate to Japan and the rest of the world how these real estate-based debt crises need to be dealt with. To take the right course of action was always going to be difficult. It would require a mix of determination not to let debt-assets gone wrong fester in bank portfolios, and a readiness to quickly organise a rescue where necessary. In the northern spring of 2007, Bear Stearns was one of the biggest investment banks on Wall Street, employing more than 14,000 people, with a book value of $97 per share and selling at a premium on book value at around $160 a share. It provided the full range of investment services, but it had something of a speciality in mortgage-backed securities. Being a thoroughly sophisticated trader, it offered all the mortgage securities-based derivatives trading that one could ask for.

Because of its place in mortgage trading, and as the notoriety of the 'sub-prime mortgage crisis' accelerated in the latter months of 2007, people began to sell Bear Stearns shares, and it finished the year trading around $100—down about 37 per cent. That should not have been a calamity. By the middle of March 2008, Australia's mortgage giant, the Commonwealth Bank, was down 39 per cent on its final 2007 price. Bear Stearns' terminal problems began in the northern spring of 2008, not so much because its shareholders were selling, but rather because its fellow traders had descended into sheer funk. Household names on Wall Street were becoming more and more terrified of mortgaged-backed securities—all, it seemed, with their fatal tranche of worthless sub-prime in the 'securitised' bundle. Bear Stearns was known to have too many of these, and eventually the bank's trading partners refused to trade with it.

In late February, the Federal Reserve rushed in with

various conduits of money for Bear Stearns, but to no avail. The Fed had to co-opt the compatible Wall Street company, J. P. Morgan, and work on Bear Stearns through Easter 2008, finally presiding over a Morgan buy-out of Bear Stearns. Apart from the incredibly cheap price of Bear Stearns (after some to-ing and fro-ing, it was sold at US$10 per share), there is nothing particularly wrong with this deal on the surface, and it may seem silly to complain about it. If Morgan and the Fed had let Bear Sterns' plummeting price continue through March unchecked, it could have set off explosions on Wall Street, evoking 1929. It was a case of breaking the downward momentum, and this was skilfully done.

Where the deal becomes a touch redolent of Japan, however, is that the Fed required, as a condition of the sale, that Bear Stearns' $30 billion portfolio of 'less than liquid assets' be kept intact. 'Less than liquid' is a euphemism for mortgage-backed securities; like the Japanese before them, the US central bankers apparently had no choice but to let expediency triumph. $30 billion in unsaleable mortgage-backed assets have been left to fester in the vaults of Bear Stearns. So the bank was holding on to billions of dollars worth of ruined stock, and possibly starting the process of the Japan syndrome. Perhaps there was no way out of this, although, to read the cries for blood in the financial blog pages of Google and *The Economist*, you could be led to think that a slash-and-burn policy might be better for us all in the long-run. But as Lord Keynes stated, 'In the long-run we are all dead'.

Where are the rest of these poisonous, empire-destroying, mortgage-backed securities with their embedded sub-prime gene? We can spy an awful lot of them outside the US banking system. David Bowers of Absolute Strategy Research said in an unpublished note to clients in March 2008 that overseas investors in America owned some $1.5 trillion of asset-backed securities that had gone badly wrong. Again, this is a case where it is not so much the actual amount that matters but the multiples that have to be strung out of it. This means trillions of dollars that will not be invested in US asset-backed securities in the future and that will not be available to fund the US current-account deficit.

For Australians, this creates a curious situation. The US dollar will depreciate against practically all currencies, and we will have shoved at us intermittently the news that the Australian dollar is rising. Against what? Against a falling US dollar. But this falling US dollar is going to require US banks to go on raising their base rate against one another. Already we have a situation where the Euro, once available for more or less nothing between US banks, now commands 4.6 per cent. So, although the Australian dollar may go on rising against the US dollar, our own excess current-account debt, which requires us to use US dollars as bank deposits, may require us to pay rising interests rates for the privilege of borrowing short-term deposit securities—even though our own currency, in the market place, could be the stronger of the two currencies. It is something further for you to rue as you contemplate the stupidity on the part of both the coalition and Labor in thwarting the household-savings revolution that Paul Keating set spinning in the 1990s.

To keep track of where America goes from here among the bewildering mass of US Federal Reserve manipulations, bailouts, US dollar-support action, liquidations, and Wall Street sharemarket gyrations, one can focus on the two institutions mentioned earlier—Fannie Mae and Freddie Mac. Put together, with well over $1.5 trillion in plain assets and more than $2 trillion in derivatives holdings, they represent a huge financial institution. And their business is, first, to buy home mortgages in the open market to keep the housing market liquid and, second, to put a guarantee on mortgages, thus allowing them to be bundled together and sold on as new securities. The extent to which Fannie Mae and Freddie Mac bundles have the poisonous sub-prime gene in them is unknown. One presumes that, as government-sponsored institutions, they would be more careful about what they obtained than other financial engineers have been.

Nonetheless, in these fevered days even the lovable Fannie and Freddie have been tarred with the same brush, and their shares—steady through the earlier part of the sub-prime crisis—found themselves plunging at the end of 2007. To steady the quality of the mortgage stock that they buy in, and thus to steady their share prices, they have had to step up the level of collateral they require on all of their mortgages. One side-effect of this will be to raise the risk of more defaults on mortgages.

NONE OF THIS adds up to an assertion that the United States is setting up the pre-requisites for a re-run of Japan. This would be a very big call indeed; it would amount to a revisiting of the Great Depression. My purpose here has been simply to reiterate what fools we mortals be, and to observe with a certain irony that, while Bernanke and his cohorts had asserted that none of the Japanese syndrome would be repeated, they have ultimately found themselves unable to avoid repeating some of it. There are enough uncertainties and time bombs out there to indicate that stagflation will run for longer than many of the market

Pollyannas say it will, but there is not enough folly evident, thus far, to threaten years of revolving Depression such as occurred in Japan. To rephrase a quote from F. Scott Fitzgerald: 'The Japanese are very different from you and me; they have a tendency to sweep problems under the rug.'

Where, then, does this leave Australia? Probably with enough problems to allow one to say that a second term for the Rudd government is no sure thing, despite what the polls say at present. All the tax cuts should have been saved. The problems, first up, are going to stem from the Australian banking system's tie to US dollar deposits. The same liquidity trap that now threatens America could well apply here. American banks are now putting a preference for liquidity above all else; and in such a situation, cutting taxes and cutting interest rates has little stimulatory effect because the banks don't want to lend. It will be surprising if something of the same does not happen here. If cost-push inflation does persist, as it is likely to, we will get slack activity, rising unemployment, and rising prices.

If you accept that this is a likely prospect, the best thing any Australian government can do is to go back and embrace the Keating revolution; put what remains of the $31 billion tax cuts into the pension-fund conduits from now on. Apart from helping to close the savings gap described earlier, it could allow us to put together a story that could be quite exciting. Go back to the beginning of the marriage between Keating's financial reforms and the triumph of the industrial pension funds. What quickly began to emerge from that were two strands of a new financial-services industry: the financing from Australia of international infrastructure, and the development of an Australian funds-management industry.

Of the two, the second may be the more promising.

Consider what has already grown out of the original Keating revolution (the combination of financial change and structural change through industrial pension funds). Between 1992 and 2007, investment funds under management in Australia grew five-fold at a compound annual growth rate of 11 per cent. The wonder of this is not so much the growth itself, but the extraordinary growth in financially skilled people here who have become capable of managing not only Australian investment funds, but also funds from throughout the Asia-Pacific region.

In recent years, Australia has become quite conclusively the largest investment-funds manager in Asia, much bigger than Japan and Singapore. The closest to us in size is Hong Kong. We have demonstrated once again the validity of the cluster theory—that if you can get a critical mass of people in a region working with a particular skill on a product, you can create an industry that elevates itself into a new dimension of value, both nationally and internationally. Perhaps the best example of this is the luxury leather-goods trade that has centred itself around Florence. There is something there now which has become unapproachable by others in skill, value, and creativity. The rest of the world beats a pathway to its door.

Australia is at the beginning—past take-off point—in creating such a cluster in assets-funds management. A cadre of people has grown up eager to delve into what is happening financially, and between them are creating a wider dimension of skills. Measured as wealth added after costs of production, the finance industry is now almost equivalent to agriculture and mining combined.

We stand now at a point of incomplete revolution. Nothing is more indicative of this than the approximately 60,000 young people—less the 300 to 400 accepted—who apply unsuccessfully each year for jobs at the Macquarie Group. These are the basis for an Antipodean Venice. This would extend the remarkable blossoming of Australia's capacity to manage the world's investment funds, in combination with a demonstrated ability to successfully invest funds across the world in toll roads, airports, power utilities, water utilities, bridges across great rivers, skyways, skyscrapers, tunnels through the world's mountains, and wind farms across its plains.

To complete the revolution, we need a federal budget-led move to an industrial pensions system rising from 9 per cent of incomes to 15 per cent. We need the Rudd government to progressively complete this task through the course of the next two-and-a-half years.

Further Reading

Coggan, Philip (2008) *Guide to Hedge Funds*, Profile Books Ltd, London

Engelbourg, Saul and Bushkoff, Leonard (1996) *The Man Who Found the Money: John Stewart Kennedy and the Financing of the Western Railroads*, Michigan State University Press, East Lansing, Michigan

Evatt, H. V. (1940) *Australian Labour Leader: the Story of W. A. Holman and the Labour Movement*, Angus & Robertson, Sydney

—— (1943) *Rum Rebellion: a Study of the Overthrow of Governor Bligh by John Macarthur and the New South Wales Corp*, Angus & Robertson, Sydney

Hayden, Bill (1996) *An Autobiography*, Angus & Robertson, Sydney

Reid, Alan (1976) *The Whitlam Venture*, Hill of Content, Melbourne

Wolfe, Tom (1988) *The Bonfire of the Vanities,* Farrar, Straus Giroux, New York